Cleopatra

THE WORLD OF CLEOPATRA AND MARK ANTONY

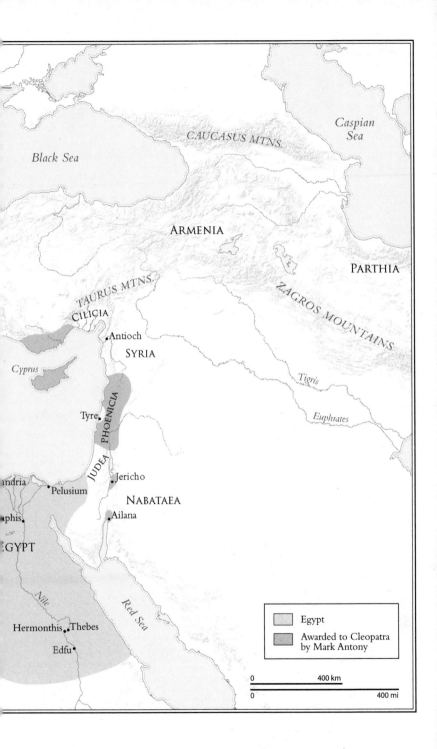

Black Sea

Caspian Sea

CAUCASUS MTNS.

ARMENIA

PARTHIA

TAURUS MTNS.

ZAGROS MOUNTAINS

CILICIA

•Antioch

SYRIA

Cyprus

Tigris

Tyre•

PHOENICIA

Euphrates

JUDEA

andria

•Pelusium

•Jericho

phis•

NABATAEA

GYPT

•Ailana

Nile

Red Sea

Hermonthis• •Thebes

Edfu•

| | Egypt |
| | Awarded to Cleopatra by Mark Antony |

0   400 km

0   400 mi

Cleopatra

Her History, Her Myth

Francine Prose

· ANCIENT LIVES ·

Yale

UNIVERSITY PRESS

NEW HAVEN & LONDON

Yale University Press books may be purchased in quantity for
educational, business, or promotional use. For information, please e-mail
sales.press@yale.edu (U.S. office) or sales@yaleup.co.uk (U.K. office).

THE AGE OF CAESAR: FIVE ROMAN LIVES by Plutarch, edited by James Romm,
translated by Pamela Mensch. Copyright © 2017 by Pamela Mensch and
James Romm. Introduction copyright © 2017 by Mary Beard.
Used by permission of W. W. Norton & Company, Inc.

Frontispiece: Beehive Mapping.

Set in the Yale typeface designed by Matthew Carter, and Louize, designed by
Matthieu Cortat, by Integrated Publishing Solutions, Grand Rapids, Michigan.
Printed in Great Britain by TJ Books Ltd, Padstow, Cornwall.

Library of Congress Control Number: 2022931893
ISBN 978-0-300-25667-3 (hardcover : alk. paper)

A catalogue record for this book is available from the British Library.

10 9 8 7 6 5 4 3 2 1

· ANCIENT LIVES ·

Ancient Lives unfolds the stories of thinkers, writers, kings, queens, conquerors, and politicians from all parts of the ancient world. Readers will come to know these figures in fully human dimensions, complete with foibles and flaws, and will see that the issues they faced — political conflicts, constraints based in gender or race, tensions between the private and public self — have changed very little over the course of millennia.

James Romm
Series Editor

The biographer must be a historian, but also a novelist and a snoop.

—Diane Johnson, *Lesser Lives*

The past is always an idea which people have about it after an event. Those whose job it is to tell the story of the past in their own present call it history. To generations born later, receiving the recollections of their parents or grandparents, or reading the historians, the past is a story, a myth handily packaged into an era, bounded by a particular event — a war, a financial crisis, a reign, a decade, a century — anything that conveniently breaks the ongoing tick of time into a manageable narrative.

—Jenny Diski, *The Sixties*

Contents

Cleopatra

Introduction

Two-thirds of the way through Plutarch's *Life of Antony* is a passage that may remind us of the ways in which close reading can broaden and deepen our understanding.

Writing more than a century after the deaths of Antony and Cleopatra, Plutarch is describing a moment when the bonds between the lovers were beginning to fray. During a long hiatus from his liaison with the Egyptian queen, Antony has married Octavia, the widowed half-sister of Octavian. Brokered by Octavian, the marriage has eased the growing tensions between the rival Roman leaders. Antony and the exemplary Octavia have been living happily in Rome, raising her two children, Antony's two sons from an earlier marriage, and two daughters whom Antony and Octavia have together. But when he sets off to fight the Parthians in Syria, Antony again longs for Cleopatra. According to Plutarch, the reawakening of that desire — the "terrible mischief" that has been slumbering — is the root cause of the catastrophic Parthian campaign in which tens of thousands of Antony's soldiers died of disease and starvation or were slaughtered in battle.

In the wake of this humiliating disaster, Antony fights his way through Armenia to the Mediterranean coast, where he summons Cleopatra to join him. She agrees but fears that Octavia is also headed there from Greece. Both women are bringing massive quantities of supplies for Antony's army. This is when the revelatory passage occurs: an account of Cleopatra's actions when for the first time she worries that she will be forced to deal with a romantic rival.

> Cleopatra, sensing that Octavia was coming to challenge her at close quarters, feared that if her rival added to the nobility of her character and the power of Caesar the pleasure of her companionship and her devotion to Antony, she would become irresistible and acquire complete mastery over her husband. So she pretended to be madly in love with Antony herself, and made herself slender by a light diet. Her glance, when he entered the room, was rapturous, and when he left, seemed downcast and despondent. She took care to be often seen weeping, and then would quickly wipe the tears away and try to conceal them, as if she wished him to be unaware of them.

The attentive reader will be struck by the fact that Cleopatra's anxious jealousy of Octavia has become an integral part of her story, an element that will figure in subsequent dramatizations of her life, from Shakespeare's *Antony and Cleopatra* to the bloated 1963 epic starring Elizabeth Taylor. What makes this fact so problematic is the tone and the substance of Plutarch's account, which—again upon close reading—will probably make us wonder, How could Plutarch have known that Cleopatra was faking her passion for Antony?

The Egyptian queen was an intelligent and diplomatic woman, who certainly would have realized that it would have been unwise to confide, even in her handmaids, the fact that she was playacting. Either Plutarch invented his interpretation of the queen's show of anguish or he was drawing on one of the primary sources that have been lost to us. What is inarguable is that either he or his source was hostile enough to Cleopatra to suspect her of fraudulence and to reject the possibility that her emotions might have been real.

I cite this passage early on in this book for the clarity and the efficiency with which it telegraphs a theme that will recur throughout: what it has meant for our understanding of Cleopatra to have had her story—her history—so often told by writers who had a political agenda, by authors who distrusted her motives, by chroniclers who were suspicious of her public and private behavior, and by historians who, to put it bluntly, believed that she was a liar.

It would be too easy to suggest that this degraded view of Cleopatra was limited to the men who told her story. The few women who took her history on were until relatively recently no less unfriendly.

In her *Lives of Cleopatra and Octavia,* written in 1757, for example, Sarah Fielding, sister of the more famous author of *Tom Jones,* writes what purports to be Cleopatra's first-person account. Cleopatra confesses to having pretended to be frightened (and in need of male protection) after she trips and stumbles upon meeting Antony at Tarsus. Her falseness is hardly surprising when, as Fielding has Cleopatra tell us, she "looked upon the rest of Mankind with the utmost Contempt; I considered them as no more capable of Feeling, then if they were inanimate.—The Pleasures or Pains of others were to me of so little Importance, that I lived as if I had been the only Creature on Earth who had any Sensation."

Any attempt to write the life of Cleopatra requires us to tease out what happened, or what is most likely to have happened, from the vision of duplicity, reckless decadence, and sluttish immorality that for a variety of reasons her contemporaries and successors have chosen to portray.

The myth that has come to surround Cleopatra has been woven over the armature of the dates and facts that can be proven. We know that she was the last ruler who belonged to the Ptolemaic dynasty, established in the wake of Alexander the Great's conquest of Egypt. We know who her father was and the names of her siblings, though there is some disagreement about how many she had. We know that three and quite likely four of her siblings died violent deaths. We know that she was highly educated and multilingual. We know — or at least we are reasonably certain — that she grew up in the vast complex of the royal palace at Alexandria.

We know what year she ascended the Egyptian throne. We know that she waged a bitter civil war against a younger brother, who was also her co-regent and spouse, a conflict that she won with the help of Julius Caesar, her lover and the father of her oldest son.

We know that she had four children, a daughter and three sons.

We know that she ruled Egypt for more than twenty years and fended off the territorial aggressions of the Roman Empire. We know that she initiated ambitious building projects, contributed to the architectural glories and intellectual life of the city of Alexandria, expanded her country's borders, and weathered a succession of serious domestic and international crises. We know that she had three children with Mark Antony. We know that she and Antony were defeated by Octavian at the Battle of Actium, after which she and Antony became bitterly estranged.

We know that her last months were desperate, as she tried to survive, hold on to her country and safeguard her children. We know she died in 30 BCE, a suicide. We know that in the immediate aftermath of her death, the Roman leader Octavian annexed Egypt — an outcome that Cleopatra had struggled to prevent during much of her reign.

Her life can be seen as a feminist story, if only because it includes so much that women were not supposed to do. Even today it would be unusual for anyone, especially a woman, to function as a city planner, military strategist, diplomat, linguist — and ruler of an enormous country with a diverse and restive population. There had been other Egyptian queens. During the fifteenth century BCE, Hatshepsut remained in power for twenty years. Like Cleopatra, she supervised heroic construction projects and enlarged Egypt's borders. Arsinoe II ruled alongside her husband-brother, Ptolemy II, against whom she conspired with her sons, two of whom were murdered. But none of Cleopatra's female predecessors have acquired a legendary status anywhere near her own.

The length and accomplishments of her reign are even more striking given the (perhaps needless to say) male-dominated era in which she lived. While Egyptian women were entitled to own property, run a business, and enjoy a certain degree of autonomy, their Greek and Roman counterparts were legally prohibited from doing almost anything without their male guardians' permission. As the historian Sarah Pomeroy notes,

> The weakness and light-mindedness of the female sex (*infirmitas sexus* and *levitas animi*) were the underlying principles of Roman legal theory that mandated all women to be under the custody of males. In childhood, a daughter fell under the sway of the eldest male ascendant in her family, the *pater familias*. The power of the *pater familias* was

without parallel in Greek law; it extended to determination of life or death for all members of the household. . . . A guardian was required when a woman performed important transactions.

Even as we argue for the recognition of how much Cleopatra accomplished, of a career that extended far beyond and encompassed far more than her love life, the irony is that much of what we know about her has come down to us because she was romantically and politically involved with two men who interested Plutarch. The most well-known and enduring narrative stories about the life of Cleopatra come from Plutarch's *Life of Antony* and, to a lesser degree, his *Life of Caesar.* Not even the nominal subject of his *Life of Antony,* Cleopatra enters it, commandeers it, proves herself to be braver and more determined than Antony, and ultimately outlives him in the text, as she did – if only briefly – in life.

Written on the cusp of the first and second centuries CE, Plutarch's *Lives* are remarkably entertaining, propelled by striking and memorable details, inspired flights of narrative, explorations of virtues and vices. They give us that sense we get from the great writers of the past of being in the presence of a human being talking directly to us.

The first time Cleopatra appears in Plutarch's *Life of Antony,* she is introduced with a sly little joke about gender and power. Plutarch is describing Fulvia, Antony's first wife, to whom he was famously unfaithful with Cleopatra. Fulvia was an unusual woman, uninterested in domesticity or the traditional female pursuits. Hungry for political influence, she tried to obtain it in the only way that a Roman matron could, by dominating a powerful man. She "wished to rule a ruler and command a commander."

Plutarch remarks that Cleopatra should have paid Fulvia tuition for teaching Antony to obey a woman – his point being that listening to a woman was so unnatural, so *unmanly* that a military hero like Antony would have needed instruction in how to do it: "Cleopatra, since she took him over tamed, and trained from the outset to obey a woman, owed a large tuition to Fulvia for having schooled Antony in the dominion of women."

That (ultimately fatal) surrender to the "dominion of women" was the sin for which Plutarch and later writers would never forgive Antony, even if Shakespeare made his audience see at least some of what so obsessed the Roman general. The concessions and mistakes that Antony made, the whittling away of his agency and manhood, the blindness he suffered on account of Cleopatra— all these are at the heart of the cautionary tale that Plutarch has set out to tell, and that was told and retold for nearly two thousand years afterward. Cleopatra's Roman detractors viewed her as a two-pronged threat: a challenge to the prevailing ideas about what a woman should be and a stubborn ruler who subverted and forestalled Rome's plans for imperial expansion and dominance.

Though the classics remind us that certain aspects of human nature and behavior are timeless, we can't help reading these works through the lens of our own era. Our current moment shapes our view of a time in which racism, imperialism, and misogyny converged in all the appalling ways in which these forces have come together. We can no longer look at the life of Cleopatra as we might have a half-century ago. Today we are aware of how her history has been told by writers who, knowingly or not, were apologists for Roman imperial expansion.

Ignoring the spectacular evidence of Egypt's history and civilization, Roman writers often portrayed Egyptians as inferior, less highly evolved: dishonest, licentious, violent, with exotic, off-putting customs. In *The Alexandrian War,* thought to have been written by Hirtius, one of Caesar's consuls, we read that "Caesar was very well aware that the Alexandrians were a deceitful people, always keeping one aim in view and pretending to another." Diodorus Siculus, a contemporary of Cleopatra's, records the story of a Roman citizen lynched by an Egyptian mob because he had accidentally killed a sacred cat. Diodorus went on to say that in times of famine, Egyptians would sooner eat one another than their pets. He marveled at the ceremonial feeding of hawks and cats, the elaborate mummification process that preserved the bodies of the sacred animals, and the lengths to which people went to deny any personal responsibility for killing a dog they had found dead in the street. He describes the delicious food served to the crocodiles, goats, bulls, and lions: "the finest wheaten flour or wheat-groats seethed in milk, every kind of sweetmeat made with honey and the meat of ducks, either boiled or baked" (book 1). Diodorus theorizes, somewhat unconvincingly, that animal worship began when the Egyptians won battles in which they flew pennants decorated with images of animals, and then concluded that the animals had arranged their victories.

When the Romans compared themselves to people who valued a cat's life above a man's, when they contrasted the modest, obedient, domestic Roman woman with the decadent, wanton Egyptian queen, they saw not only an economic and strategic but also a moral imperative for annexing Egypt.

Though Cleopatra was born—and apparently thought of herself as—a Macedonian Greek, all that mattered to her Roman contemporaries was that she was not a Roman and, more important, that her existence, her influence, and her power constituted an obstacle to Roman expansion. She was a force to be destroyed or encouraged to destroy herself so that the empire could prevail. Her gender, her exoticized "Easternness," and her determination to protect her country's autonomy helped explain why Egypt was thought to need the moral, political, and practical guidance of Rome — and why Cleopatra did in fact need the support and allegiance of Mark Antony and Julius Caesar.

It is hard not to notice how profoundly her gender determined the way in which her story has been told. Despite the evidence of her achievements — the kingdom she ruled, the city she helped build, the seeming ease with which she navigated between the two worlds of Rome and Egypt — she is generally better known for seducing, managing, and manipulating her Roman lovers, Julius Caesar and Mark Antony.

The Romans were the first of many to depict Cleopatra as a cruel Asiatic queen, all greedy ambition and no moral conscience. Alexandre Cabanel's 1887 orientalist painting, *Cleopatra Testing Poisons on Condemned Prisoners,* shows the queen lounging on her sofa as prisoners — guinea pigs for her testing of deadly toxins — die in agony around her. The story of a woman who recklessly destroys men, or who is responsible for our eternal exile from the Garden of Eden, or who incites a ruthless murder or a catastrophic war has never gone out of fashion.

The visceral horror of ambitious women is evident in this extraordinary passage from Plutarch about Olympias, the mother of Alexander the Great. "Once a serpent was seen stretched out next to the body of Olympias as she slept, and this, more than anything else, they say, abated the ardor of Philip's passion for her. Accordingly, he no longer came often to sleep next to her, either because he feared she might cast a magic spell on him, or thought she was the familiar of some superior being."

The language of charms, spells, and enchantment likewise surrounds Cleopatra in Plutarch's *Lives,* and the work of those who borrowed from him. When these men write that Cleopatra's magic turned Mark Antony into her plaything, they do not mean it metaphorically. They mean that she practiced magic, which made her power inexplicable, unpredictable, unfair. They mean that she had a shortcut, a way to function without the more admirable skills and virtues — diplomacy, courage, political and military savvy — that would be required of a man in her position.

Writing in the first century CE, Propertius uses Cleopatra as an example of the kind of evil witch who employs her vile tricks to enslave a man; he cites mythical women like Medea, Penthesilea, and Semiramis, forebears of his own beloved and despised Cynthia, the name by which the poet refers to the heartless woman who inspired his *Elegies*. What enraged Propertius was not only the so-called licentiousness of Cleopatra, "that whore, queen of incestuous Canopus," but her political and cultural ambitions: her attempt to elevate the jackal-headed Egyptian deity Anubis over the Roman god Jupiter, to subjugate the importance of the Tiber to that of the Nile, to replace the Roman trumpet with the sistrum (an Egyptian musical instrument), and to "spread her foul mosquito nets over the Tarpeian Rock," a cliff that abutted the Capitoline Hill.

The poet praises Octavian, later crowned as the emperor Augustus, for having saved Rome, and addresses the vanquished queen, taunting her about her suicide: "You fled to the wandering mouths of the frightened Nile. . . . I saw your arms bitten by asps and your limbs draw sleep in by a secret path."

To Horace, born at about the same time as Octavian, she was a "baleful marvel." One of Horace's most famous odes, written soon after Cleopatra's death, celebrates the defeat of the "inflamed" queen's plot against Rome and the burning of her ships, though it ends with a nod to the courage and resolve with which she resisted capture, exile, and public humiliation. "But with a countenance serene could eye / Her ruined palace, and courageously / Handle infuriate asps, nor shrank / While their foul spume her body drank: / Firmer since she her death had pre-ordained, / Not she, in truth, by rude Liburnians deigned / To be borne off triumphantly, / As though some low-born woman, she."

In his *Pharsalia* (*Civil War*), composed during the mid-first century CE, Lucan tells the story of Cleopatra at some length. Like other classical authors, he emphasized the political threat that she posed when "Egypt's shame" dared to test "whether a woman *not of our race* [emphasis mine] might rule the world," a trial launched when this "wanton daughter of the Ptolemies" arrived "to pollute a Roman general's bed." Even in translation, the language of racial pollution speaks clearly.

For those early writers whose attention she captured, her sexuality and her talents as a seductress defined her: "Who can refuse to pardon Mark Antony's wild infatuation, when even Caesar's unfeeling heart took fire," asked Lucan, adding, "He tainted his thoughts with adulterous lust, mixed illicit lovemaking, bastard offspring with the affairs of war. . . . She would have sought to sway Caesar's hard heart in vain, if her beauty had not added to her prayers, and lust pleaded for her."

The witchy, seductive Egyptian, a racist misogynist paradigm, was eagerly adopted and amplified by later authors. Over time, Cleopatra descended from what she was in life — an intelligent and competent ruler at a perilous moment in her country's history — into the personification of everything Eastern, decadent, and female, a despot who spent and squandered a fortune and cast her blinding spell over two Roman heroes. Writing in the fourteenth century, Boccaccio tells us that she "ensnared that lustful man with her beauty and wanton eyes" and "kept him wretchedly in love with her." In the early seventeenth century, a forged volume of pornography, *Letters on the Infamous Libido of Cleopatra the Queen*, included an account, allegedly written by Mark Antony, of how the libidinous queen put on a hood and had sex with 106 men in a brothel.

Not only was Cleopatra's power (especially her influence over her lovers) considered hazardous and unseemly, but she was viewed as a victim of pathological lust, or, to use a word thankfully out of fashion today, a nymphomaniac. Like other famous "witches" — Circe, Medea — she was the personification of the male fear of, and distaste for, unfettered female sexuality.

Since the abilities with which Plutarch and his successors credit Cleopatra were limited to one skill set, seduction, it is not surprising that so much attention has been focused on her appearance. The famous passage in Shakespeare's *Antony and Cleopatra* ("Age cannot wither her, not custom stale") is a hymn to the vitality of certain older women, while the well-known lines from Plutarch suggest that her beauty was outshone by her brilliance and charm: "For her actual beauty, it is said, was not, in and of itself, utterly beyond compare, or such as to astound those who beheld her; but her presence cast an inescapable spell, and her appearance, combined with the persuasiveness of her talk, and the personality that suffused all she said and did, had something bewitching about it."

Perhaps a physical image of the queen survived into Plutarch's time, but it is unlikely that Shakespeare had any idea what she looked like. Nor do we. Except for a rough likeness of her face on some crudely fashioned coins, there is no portrait of her that we fully trust. Sculptures in the Vatican, in Berlin, and in Rome's Capitoline Museum are said to represent Cleopatra, but none of them has ever been (and none may ever be) satisfactorily authenticated.

She may well have been beautiful. But her beauty is a construct that writers and historians have based on the assumption that only a very beautiful woman, ideally one with access to magic, could have charmed two of her era's most influential and powerful military and political leaders. Her allure so clouded her Roman lovers' better judgment that at the risk of alienating their supporters and threatening their careers, Julius Caesar and Mark Antony went to considerable trouble to spend time with her in Rome and Alexandria, and Antony repeatedly called for her to join him in the midst of military campaigns.

If we view Cleopatra through any lens except that of her appearance, her seductiveness, her sexual agency, and her relationships with two men, we see a brave and highly competent leader. Revered as a living goddess, she was an accomplished diplomat and military strategist. She helped maintain Alexandria as one of the ancient world's most vibrant and beautiful cities, even as she made the complicated decisions and carried out the duties of ruling a multilingual, multicultural state with a vast bureaucracy and perpetual ethnic and class tensions between Egyptians and the Macedonian Greeks, dividing the peasants from the priests and from the officials who oppressed them. It was not just an abstract achievement but a political survival skill to have mastered as many languages as Plutarch tells us Cleopatra spoke.

The only existing document believed to have been signed by Cleopatra herself concerns a matter of customs and tax exemptions for one of Mark Antony's generals. Daily life must have included many such signings and minor obligations, though we have been encouraged to think, as so many Romans and their successors seemed to believe, that she passed her time getting dressed, applying cosmetics, concocting love potions, and plotting erotic conquests. It is hard to think of a king or emperor whose prodigious achievements and accomplishments were so widely ignored even as he was ferociously reviled for having conducted two sequential and serious love affairs.

According to the historians W. W. Tarn and M. P. Charlesworth, Cleopatra has inspired "one of the most terrible outbursts of hatred in history; no accusation was too vile to be hurled at her." Much has been made of the jeweled pleasure boat, the gilded palace, of the waste and excess in which she indulged while ordinary Egyptians went hungry. The Egyptian priests and the Macedonian ruling class might have argued that the splendor was proper and even necessary for a queen who, like her Ptolemaic forebears, was part human, part divine, but that would have seemed heretical to the Romans, who prided themselves on their (relative) temperance and republican ideals.

For the writers and readers who lived after her, her successive liaisons with Caesar and Antony have overshadowed the fact that for more than two decades a woman outwitted her political enemies while successfully thwarting the acquisitive Roman Empire. The speed and thoroughness with which Octavian absorbed Cleopatra's kingdom after her death offered yet more evidence that in its final decades Egypt had owed its (relative) independence and survival largely to its last Ptolemaic queen.

Cleopatra's legend has inspired writers from disparate cultures and distant historical periods to focus on her alleged licentiousness, her elaborately staged seductions, and, even more dramatically, her suicide, allegedly by snakebite. Only in recent decades have historians attempted to construct from the available fragments a fuller, less constricted narrative of her life.

A more accurate picture might be formed by adding to these narratives of sex and death a deeper appreciation for the daily labor of governance and statesmanship, the constant calculations required to regulate currency and ameliorate the effects of periodic droughts and crop failures, to pacify the powerful priests and outwit the ambitious and hostile courtiers who surrounded her. Two millennia after her death, we can only marvel at the immense responsibility and daunting challenge of remaining in power and guiding an enormous country through famine and war during two tense and difficult decades.

Meanwhile the changing (or unchanging) manners and mores that separate our time from hers can be tracked by looking at the ways in which successive centuries have portrayed her. She has become a sort of mirror in which each era sees itself. Novels have been written and epic films made; television programs about her can be streamed day and night. Among the women in antiquity, she is one of the few who has endured as an object of curiosity, fascination, and desire.

PART I

The Life of Cleopatra

CHAPTER ONE

The Ptolemaic Background

The dynasty to which Cleopatra belonged, which lasted almost three hundred years and ended with her death, was established around 330 BCE, after Alexander the Great, a Macedonian Greek, freed the country from its hated and oppressive Persian occupiers, who had conquered it ten years earlier. He was greeted as a liberator and encountered little resistance.

While in control of Egypt, Alexander endeavored to establish his connection with the ancient pharaonic dynasties. He made a ceremonial visit to the temple at Memphis and arranged to have himself crowned pharaoh at the shrine of Ptah, the Egyptian god of creation. This temple would remain a center of Egyptian religious life, even after the capital was moved to Alexandria.

Finally, Alexander consulted the oracle at the Siwa Oasis in the Libyan desert. According to some reports, the oracle proclaimed that Alexander was not only the ruler of the world but also the son of the Egyptian god Ammon, a deity often conflated with Zeus in an early commingling of Egyptian and Greek religions.

Oracular pronouncements and prophecies were extremely important in Egyptian culture, and the oracle's approval of the Macedonian conqueror established the legitimacy of his authority. Though the melding of Greek and Egyptian religion would be encouraged by the Ptolemaic rulers — statues of the Egyptian gods were erected in Alexandria — there is evidence that the equation between the deities of the two cultures had begun much earlier. As early as the fifth century BCE, Herodotus tried to locate an Egyptian equivalent for each Greek god.

Earlier, Alexander had founded a new city on the site of an Egyptian village on the Mediterranean coast, ideally suited as a harbor that could be accessed from the Nile. In 331 he named the new city Alexandria and hired architects, builders, and urban planners to construct the structures and lay out the broad streets. The public squares were organized according to a plan that he himself designed.

According to Diodorus Siculus, "By selecting the right angle of the streets, Alexander made the city breathe with the etesian winds so that as these blow across a great expanse of the sea, they cool the air of the town, and so he provided its inhabitants with a moderate climate and good health" (book 17). (Later historians have credited the urban design to Dinocrates of Rhodes.) Centuries later, Caesar was impressed by the city's construction, as well as by the fact that its reliance on concrete and masonry and its lack of floor beams and timber made it essentially fireproof. Or at least partly fireproof; the Great Library of Alexandria was severely damaged by fire during the civil war between Cleopatra and her brother.

When Alexander died in Babylon, in 323, his generals struggled to determine how, in the absence of an heir or designated successor, his empire would be divided. His close associate and (according to some) distant relation Ptolemy emerged as the victor and laid claim to wealthy, fertile Egypt, watered by the Nile. He would later become known as Ptolemy Soter (Savior) or, to modern historians, Ptolemy I.

After successfully defending Egypt against his political and military rivals, Ptolemy became pharaoh around 305–304. He founded a dynasty that kept an ancient and important civilization alive, and for a while extended Egypt's borders to include Libya, Cyprus, Crete, Palestine, part of Syria, Crimea, and what we now know as modern Greece.

Because it was believed that Alexander the Great could not be properly worshipped while his relics lay elsewhere, Ptolemy I established his own primacy and increased the power of the political-military-religious Alexandrian cult by stealing Alexander's body as it made its way from Babylon to Egypt and having it brought to Memphis. Later, his son Ptolemy II would order the body transferred to Alexandria: one of those grisly postmortem journeys like that of Eva Perón in which ownership of a corpse was believed to confer political power.

Ptolemy I realized that one way to pacify the Greek-speaking expatriates and the Macedonian transplants, and to prevent the Egyptians from growing rebellious under foreign domination, was to encourage immigration to Egypt from Greece and at the same time convince the immigrants and the local populations that his regime was part Greek, part Egyptian. This was not, strictly speaking, true. Although they absorbed some aspects of the culture of the country they occupied, the royal family endeavored to remain linguistically, racially, and ethnically Macedonian.

Beyond the royal palace and throughout Egypt, intermarriage was common, and it was frequently hard to distinguish Greeks from Egyptians. Yet the degree of harmony between the native Egyptians and the newer immigrants from Greece fluctuated, and the tension between the indigenous population and their Hellenistic rulers persisted until – and throughout – the reign of Cleopatra.

The culture of Greece was not fully translatable since the olive trees so central to the Greek diet and daily life failed to thrive in Egyptian soil. Peaceful periods were interrupted by eras of ethnic tension during which the Greeks were seen by the native Egyptians as interlopers forcing their will on what remained of a proud, ancient civilization.

In matters of religion, the Macedonian Greeks adopted and adapted whatever seemed likely to consolidate their influence and power. The kings and queens participated in the sacrifices and ceremonies that had the largest popular followings and at which their presence would have been most visible.

In his efforts to consolidate the native and imported religions, Ptolemy I promoted the worship of Serapis, a god who combined aspects of the Egyptian god Osiris, the sacred Apis bull, and the Greek god Zeus; the deity was represented in an anthropomorphic form with the long hair and beard of a Greek god, more comprehensible and convincing to the Greeks than the animal-headed deities of the Egyptians that so discomfited Diodorus. Serapeums were built throughout Egypt, but Ptolemy III established the grandest of them on a rocky plateau overlooking Alexandria; the magnificent temple would become a popular pilgrimage site.

The Ptolemies were fortunate in having assumed control of a country accustomed to deifying and worshipping its living and dead kings and queens. The Ptolemaic rulers were accorded divine honors to deepen the connection between the temple and the state.

The blending of Greek and Egyptian cultures was not without friction. According to the historian Michel Chauveau, "The fracture line created by the massive arrival of Greeks in Egypt not only separated the two communities, it affected individuals to the point of sometimes provoking a veritable cultural schizophrenia." Though Egypt has been portrayed as an example of cultural homogenization, on the order of medieval Spain or Sicily under the Normans, Chauveau suggests a "coexistence founded on relative and mutual ignorance, like two parallel universes developing almost autonomously, with few reciprocal effects" (*Egypt in the Age of Cleopatra*).

A common thread connecting Greeks, Romans, and Egyptians was what we would call superstition, though we need to remember that what we consider magical thinking was believed by earlier civilizations to have a basis in science. Oracles, portents, omens, and dreams revealed the future with a clarity that skeptics (most famously, Julius Caesar) ignored at their own peril. Gods required sacrifices to avert disaster, to guarantee favorable weather, and to ensure military victory.

The commingling of religions worked in both directions: The cult of Isis — goddess not only of the harvest but also of human fertility, motherhood, and marriage — spread throughout the Roman Empire. It became one of the most vigorous religions in the empire, popular with both women and men who worshipped a goddess who brought forth crops and hurled lightning bolts, the restorer of life who had pieced together the butchered remains of her murdered brother and lover, Osiris, and brought him back from the dead. A temple dedicated to Isis, destroyed by an earthquake in 62 CE, rebuilt, and lost again during the eruption of Vesuvius in 79, has been discovered in the ruins of Pompeii.

At least some of Cleopatra's political power resulted from the fact that she identified herself with Isis and was worshipped as her living manifestation. She appeared at official events costumed as the goddess in a crown encircled by cobras. In the first centuries after Christ, efforts were made throughout the Roman Empire to suppress the cult of Isis and, by extension, the vestigial adoration of Cleopatra as a minor goddess.

The Egyptian passion for constructing temples and monuments was carried on by the Macedonian Greeks, under whose rule the port of Alexandria, with a population from all over the known world that included not only Greeks and Egyptians but Jews, Ethiopians, and Libyans, became a city of broad avenues, fountains, and well-tended parks, with a famous museum and the great library that attracted scholars from distant lands. Led by a succession of librarians who were minor celebrities in Alexandrian society, it was said to have contained thousands of papyrus scrolls. Historians, ancient and modern, have attempted to calculate the extent of the library's holdings. The early Ptolemies were apparently so obsessed with adding to it that they confiscated every book arriving in Alexandria, deposited it in the library, and created a copy to recompense its original owner. Early in the third century BCE, Zenodotus of Ephesus, its first librarian, organized the volumes in alphabetical order and produced new editions of the *Iliad* and *Odyssey*. Not only did the library contain the work of the most important Greek writers, but it also housed thousands of Greek translations of Egyptian, Babylonian, Persian, Phoenician, and Hebrew texts.

Another of Alexandria's famous attractions was its lighthouse, the Pharos, one of the Seven Wonders of the Ancient World. The Greek historian and geographer Strabo, who visited Alexandria in the late first century BCE, described the lighthouse: multistoried (perhaps as much as four hundred feet tall), it was made of white stone, either marble or limestone. In the next century, the satirist Lucian of Samosata imagined being up in the sky looking down at the earth, and being unable to recognize the planet until he saw the Colossus of Rhodes and the Pharos lighthouse (*Icaromenippus*).

Strabo also left an account of beauties of Alexandria's harbor, its great museum's walkways, sitting areas, and communal eating spaces, the public and sacred buildings, among them the tomb of Alexander, the law courts and the stadium, the magnificent Gymnasium, a zoo housing a range of exotic animals, and a rocky mound, artificially created, that could be climbed for a panoramic view of the harbor.

The palace that Cleopatra would one day inhabit was renowned for its size and grandeur. An earthquake and tsunami eventually submerged the entire structure beneath the ocean, where it was discovered and excavated by French archaeologists beginning in 1998. In 2010, a team of divers led by the French underwater archaeologist Franck Goddio exhibited some of the findings that had been recovered, among them a colossal head believed to represent Cleopatra's son Caesarion, as well as large and small statues of rulers and deities, coins, and everyday objects.

According to Strabo, a third of the city was given over to the area occupied by the palaces, whose occupants had a dedicated harbor for their personal use. History and poetry have given Cleopatra the ultimate symbol of luxury: the solid gold bejeweled pleasure boat in which she sailed to greet Mark Antony.

Perhaps because the idea of the great library still commands our respect, perhaps because of Strabo's enchantment with her city, Cleopatra's Alexandria can sound like a Ptolemaic paradise where scholars came to study and highly educated citizens mingled with expert editors come to work on new, improved texts of Homer. But it was also a rough-and-tumble port, crowded with an international cast of rich and poor men and women. It had a significant crime rate and a politically volatile mood that could start the population rioting, storming out from their neighborhoods and up to the gates of the palace. These problems would create yet another unstable element for Cleopatra to cope with as she tried to balance the conflicting pressures and demands of her city, her country, and the Roman Empire.

In the 1932 film *Million Dollar Legs,* set in the fictive country of Klopstokia, all the women are named Angela and all the men are named George. When the kingdom's ruler, played by W. C. Fields, is asked why the Klopstokians do this, he replies, "Why not?"

Presumably, the Ptolemaic kings had a more cogent reason for naming all their male children Ptolemy and their daughters Cleopatra, Arsinoe, or Berenice. But the result has not made things easier for the historian, who must sort out the rare peaceful successions, the rivalries and blood feuds, the sibling marriages that led to conspiracy, civil war, and murder. Partly helpful is the fact that many of the rulers were given nicknames: Mother Lover, Father Lover, Sister Lover, Fatty, Chickpea, and the Bastard.

In the spring of 282 BCE, Ptolemy I died and was succeeded by his son Ptolemy II, who waged war against the rulers of Syria and Nubia and expanded the borders of the Egyptian Empire, colonizing the coast of the Red Sea and clearing a waterway between the Nile and the sea, a precursor of the Suez Canal. Under his leadership, Egypt became a significant naval power.

Ptolemy II was the first of the Ptolemaic leaders to practice sibling marriage. Though initially regarded by the Greeks as a form of incest, marriage between siblings came to seem a convenient way to ensure the "purity" of the Macedonian line and preempt conflicting ambitions at court. In addition, it reconciled the relatively high status of Egyptian women with the relative servitude of women in Greece. In practice, marriages between brothers and sisters were often disastrous, the cause of brutal family murders in nearly every generation.

After repudiating his first wife, Arsinoe I, who had been accused of plotting against him, Ptolemy II, according to Chauveau, "managed a propaganda coup on behalf of his dynasty by marrying his own sister, Arsinoe II, and by treating her death as an opportune apotheosis. The cult of the new goddess Philadelphos made it possible to unite Greeks and Egyptians in a common loyalistic fervor, thus assuring the long-term attachment of his subjects to his line" (*Egypt in the Age of Cleopatra*). The cult dedicated to Arsinoe would become extremely popular. Ptolemy II also worked to intensify the religious devotion to Alexander the Great, who was honored with officially sponsored rites. And Ptolemy also deified his parents and numerous other relatives, established an elaborate annual festival in honor of his father, and ordered the construction and restoration of temples throughout Egypt.

In 246, Ptolemy II was succeeded by Ptolemy III, the son of his father's first wife. He was the first of the Ptolemaic pharaohs to be threatened by — and to suppress — a revolt by Egyptians whose sufferings had been increased by a disastrous famine and the taxes levied to support the foreign wars that further expanded Egypt's territory. In addition to ordering the construction of the Serapeum at Alexandria, Ptolemy III continued the tradition, begun by his father and grandfather, of building temples and encouraging scholarship and literature.

The reigns of Ptolemy II and Ptolemy III were arguably the dynasty's most stable and successful periods. New irrigation projects were initiated, agricultural reforms put in place. An elaborate administrative system was established to oversee craft production, taxation, and the revenue generated by the profitable export of grain and papyrus. The end to the Persian occupation and the advent of (relative) peace and prosperity had nurtured a cultural renaissance and the flowering of the city of Alexandria at that culture's center.

The years — nearly two centuries, in fact — of decline began with

Ptolemy III's son and successor, Ptolemy IV, who was notable partly for the violence of his regime, in particular the intrafamilial murderousness that blighted nearly every successive generation of the Ptolemaic dynasty and that would persist until (and include) the reign of Cleopatra.

The litany of Ptolemaic family horrors is so long, complex, and awful that historians and biographers have often adopted an almost comically neutral tone as they rattle off the crimes. Here is Stacy Schiff on the subject of Cleopatra's heritage: "In the late third century, [Ptolemy IV] murdered his uncle, mother and brother. Courtiers saved him from poisoning his wife by doing so themselves, once she had produced an heir. Over and over mothers sent troops against sons. Sisters waged war against brothers. Cleopatra's great-grandmother fought one civil war against her parents, a second against her children. . . . Berenice II's mother borrowed Berenice's foreign-born husband, for which double-duty Berenice supervised his murder. . . . Cleopatra III . . . was born the wife and niece of Ptolemy VIII. He raped her when she was an adolescent, at which time he was simultaneously married to her mother. The two quarreled. Ptolemy killed their fourteen-year-old son, chopped him up into pieces, and delivered a chest of mutilated limbs to the palace gates on her birthday."

Of course, the custom of murdering close relatives was not exclusive to Ptolemaic Egypt. It persisted in Europe at least through the Elizabethan Age, and is still practiced in places where dictatorships and strong monarchies incite and reward homicidal transfers of power. It does make one rethink our notions of family and how we treat those close to us. It reminds us of how foolish it is to assume that we can fully understand the thoughts, emotions, and instincts of those who lived in a another era — human beings with such different worldviews that even such (one would think) basic institutions as the family have little in common from era to era except the facts of blood and birth.

Family violence seems to have been prevalent not only in the royal palace. When Diodorus Siculus, the Greek historian who lived around the time of Julius Caesar and died the same year as Cleopatra, writes about the laws of the Egyptians, it is not entirely clear which legal system he means, since laws varied from city to country, region to region. Still striking is this passage suggesting that familial violence was not restricted to kings and queens, though pharaohs were exempt from the harsh and peculiar laws he describes:

> In the case of parents who had slain their children . . . the offenders had to hold the dead body in their arms for three successive days and nights, under the surveillance of a state guard; for it was not considered just to deprive of life those who had given life to their children. . . . But for children who had killed their parents they reserved an extraordinary punishment; for it was required that those found guilty of this crime should have pieces of flesh about the size of a finger cut out of their bodies with sharp reeds and then be put on a bed of thorns and burned alive; for they held that to take by violence the life of those who had given them life was the greatest crime possible to man. (Book 1.)

But in addition to arranging to have his brother scalded in his bath and his mother poisoned, Ptolemy IV was obliged to contend with another rebellion.

Once more, the burdensome taxation system and the inequalities of power and land ownership had inspired opposition to the pharaoh, and the army that had been raised to fight against Syria turned against the Ptolemies. The indigenous rebels won the support of the priestly class. The pharaoh lost control of Upper Egypt, so much so that at his death the south of the country seceded from the rest.

The country remained divided until Ptolemy V ascended the throne in 205 BCE, and reconquered Thebes and the Nile Delta. During these years, Egypt lost a large amount of territory to its near neighbors. The expenses and distractions of waging foreign wars and putting down internal revolts prevented the pharaoh from continuing the ambitious construction projects that the earlier Ptolemies had initiated, and it has been said that the empire's decline and the resultant weaknesses that would create political difficulties—vis à vis Rome—for Cleopatra began during this period. Eventually, Ptolemy V was able to broker a peace with Syria by marrying the daughter of Antiochus III, Syria's Macedonian ruler, the descendant of another of Alexander's generals.

This daughter would be crowned Cleopatra I, named after Alexander's sister. When she inherited the throne in 180, after the death of her husband, she was, in theory, serving as regent for her young son, but in fact she was the sole ruler of the country, and she established the rights and privileges that so affected the lives of Egyptian women, who frequently were well educated, could marry, divorce, and travel at will, and were empowered to inherit property in their own name and participate in legal proceedings.

Age six at the time of his father's death, Ptolemy VI ruled under his mother's regency and in consort with his sister and his brother Ptolemy VII, whom he later expelled from the country. The wars with Syria resumed; Ptolemy VI was exiled by another brother, Ptolemy VIII, and sent to live in Cyprus, from which he eventually returned to retake the kingdom.

After Ptolemy VI died while fighting in Syria, Ptolemy VIII, nicknamed Physcon, or "Fatty," assumed control of the country and cemented a stronger relationship with Rome than his predecessors had enjoyed, eventually being declared a "friend and ally of the Roman people" – and thus endangering Egypt's sovereignty. Ptolemy launched a purge of those who had supported his younger brother and, allegedly, a massacre in which innocent Alexandrians were killed apparently at random. Among the murdered were a number of intellectuals. Other scholars and literary figures were sent into exile, and the stewardship of the great library was entrusted to one of the pharaoh's military cronies – thus contributing to the decline of Alexandrian culture.

When Fatty died in 116, his son, Ptolemy IX – "Chickpea" – ruled the country together with his mother and grandmother. After his mother claimed that he had tried to have her assassinated and had his younger brother Ptolemy X installed as ruler, Ptolemy IX retreated to Cyprus, from which he eventually returned and reclaimed the Egyptian throne.

During his reign, Ptolemy X had become deeply indebted to Roman financiers. In his will, as collateral against a loan that had enabled him to defeat a rebel army, he bequeathed his country to Rome in the event that he died without a male heir. This foolish gesture was to have lasting consequences. Though Rome never directly attempted to enforce the provisions of the will, the document highlighted Egypt's vulnerability and its financial dependence on Rome. The Roman view of Egypt as a source of extractable wealth would grow more pervasive, its requests for tributes more demanding. This situation would be greatly exacerbated during the reign of Cleopatra's father, Ptolemy XII.

In 80 BCE, the Roman dictator Lucius Cornelius Sulla installed Ptolemy XI on the Egyptian throne after insisting that the new ruler marry his much older stepmother. When the Egyptian king agreed, then promptly murdered his new bride, he was killed by the people of Alexandria, who had preferred the wife he had executed.

Next in the line of succession was the pharaoh's brother, Ptolemy of Cyprus, who committed suicide rather than surrender Cyprus to Rome, as he knew he would be asked to do. This death would assume a mythic significance for the remaining Ptolemies, and when Antony later included Cyprus among his gifts to Cleopatra, it would have been considered a restitution of land that was rightfully hers—as well as a correction of a wrong that had been done to her family.

After the death of Ptolemy of Cyprus, Cleopatra's father, Ptolemy XII, was recalled to Egypt. Though he was illegitimate, the son of Ptolemy IX and a concubine, he was the only remotely suitable dynastic heir and therefore the sole hope of keeping Rome at bay. He was soon appointed king. This was done partly with the idea of thwarting Sulla, who had designs on Egypt. That threat came even closer to being implemented after Sulla died and was replaced by Pompey, the Roman general who had annexed Judea, bringing the empire's border right up to that of Egypt.

Ptolemy XII was nicknamed the Bastard (a reference to his illegitimacy) and Auletes, the Flute Player, a derisive title derived from the widespread joke about his leadership qualities: it was said that he would rather play his flute than rule Egypt. The New Dionysus was the name that Ptolemy XII chose for himself: the name of a Greek god, a lover of pleasure and wine. Auletes was said to have presided over orgiastic celebrations in the royal palace, feasts that involved music, wild drunkenness, and dancing.

The cult of Dionysus had long been popular in Rome, and a statue of the god decorated Julius Caesar's villa on the west bank of the Tiber—a house where Cleopatra would later stay as Caesar's guest. In Egypt, Dionysus had increasingly become identified with Osiris, the god of fertility, of the dead, and of resurrection. Dionysus is also what people would later call Mark Antony. When Cleopatra arrived in her golden barge for their fateful meeting, Plutarch writes, "A rumor spread everywhere that Aphrodite had come to revel with Dionysus for the good of Asia." But Antony's profligate ways also reminded Plutarch of the god's two faces: "Dionysus, the Giver of Joy, and the Gentle. And so indeed he was to some, but to far more the Raw-Eater and the Savage." One wonders which Dionysus Auletes intended by taking the name, the happy god or the ferocious deity — or whether he meant both.

During Auletes' reign, he essentially mortgaged the Egyptian economy in return for the influence and support he secured from Rome. At the time of his death, he was in debt for 17.5 million drachmas: the cost of the lavish banquets he had hosted in pursuit of Roman support and the absurdly generous gifts he had given his allies, among them the golden crown he presented to Pompey. At one of Auletes' feasts, a thousand guests were each given a new gold cup for each course and encouraged to take them home.

In 59, Pompey, Caesar, and Crassus — who together had formed the First Triumvirate — agreed to support the Egyptian king in return for a fee to be paid by Ptolemy XII, a price that the historian Michael Grant has estimated as being worth half the entire revenue of Egypt for six months, or possibly a year.

Despite the extraordinary expense, the bargain represented something of a rescue and a reprieve, since Pompey and Caesar had been eyeing the annexation of Egypt with increasing eagerness. Even so, the Egyptians were predictably unhappy about the debt and the taxes imposed to pay it.

Taxes have always been a heated subject for the people who pay them, and in Ptolemaic Egypt periods of unrest often began as an expression of rage at the excessive rates. The idea of being exorbitantly taxed to pay for the golden cups that their pharaoh had given his Roman guests was finally too much. The unfair tax burden, the financial instability, and the perceived inattentiveness of Auletes' leadership inspired a new outbreak of rioting. Ptolemy fled the unrest in Alexandria and found refuge in Rome. It has been suggested that Cleopatra, age nine or ten, accompanied her father on this journey, which would have been her first trip to Rome.

Auletes' long absence from home and his stay in Pompey's luxurious villa in the Alban Hills did little to quiet the rage and unrest in Alexandria. When a party of over a hundred envoys arrived from Egypt to Rome to inform the pharaoh of his country's displeasure with him, and of the people's desire that he go into permanent exile and leave Egypt to his daughter Berenice IV (Cleopatra's older sister), Ptolemy had the head envoy and many of the messengers killed.

The alliance between the Romans and the Egyptians was no more popular in Rome than it was in Alexandria. A series of evil omens—lightning struck a statue of Jupiter in the Alban Hills, presumably near Pompey's villa—were interpreted as warnings about the dangers and difficulties that would be incurred if Rome continued to support the Egyptian king. Pompey should have taken these portents more seriously, since his alliance with Egypt would ultimately bring about his death. The Romans expressed their disapproval by rioting in the streets, even as their counterparts were rioting in Egypt. The Roman-Egyptian alliance seemed to have been popular mostly with those parties who stood to make a profit or engineer a regime change.

In Auletes' absence, the power vacuum inspired Berenice to crown herself queen of Egypt in 56. After a husband was found for the queen, she arranged to have him strangled days after the marriage. Her rebellion now meant that Auletes was obliged to add, to his existing debt, the astronomical cost of transporting and maintaining the mercenary army that would help him take back the throne.

Leading Auletes' campaign against Berenice was Aulus Gabinius, a Roman general and an ally of Pompey. With Gabinius's help, and that of his ferocious and unruly army—the Gabiniani, many of whom were of Germanic and Gallic descent—Ptolemy XII returned to Egypt, executed Berenice, and regained the throne in 55 BCE.

CHAPTER TWO

A Transfer of Power

In the months that followed the 2020 U.S. election, the world became newly aware of the importance of a peaceful transfer of power: how with maximum efficiency and minimal disruption one leader succeeds another. It is a ritual, a necessity, an end and a beginning. At the highest level, the most orderly change is a minor cataclysm.

One deceptively smooth transition occurred in 51 BCE, when Ptolemy XII died of natural causes. There is some confusion about the precise date of Auletes' death. It seems to have been one of those scenarios, like the plot of Akira Kurosawa's brilliant film *Kagemusha,* in which a court scrambles in secret to devise some plan of action before the people are informed that the samurai lord is dead.

The Flute Player's peaceful death was a rare occurrence in the history of the Ptolemaic dynasty, whose leaders had been strangling, poisoning, and dismembering one another for the previous three hundred years. Four years earlier, Auletes had ensured his own relatively tranquil demise by executing his daughter Berenice, thus eliminating his principal rival for control of the country.

The staggering debts that Auletes had incurred, Egypt's growing dependence on Rome, the widespread corruption among the Egyptian administrators and the priestly class, and the resultant economic and political instability comprised the legacy inherited by his second daughter, Cleopatra VII, who at the time of his death was eighteen.

Little is known about the years that preceded Cleopatra's coronation, but in her 2010 biography *Cleopatra*, Stacy Schiff provides a persuasive sketch of the queen's childhood: a wet nurse, games in the palace, trips to Memphis for religious festivals, a rigorous multilingual education, an easy familiarity with the works of Homer and the glorious library of Alexandria.

The vagueness of our knowledge about the queen's early years is compounded by our uncertainty about her mother's identity. The historian Duane W. Roller has suggested that Cleopatra's mother was part Macedonian, as well as a member of the priestly family of Ptah, which meant that Cleopatra was three-quarters Macedonian and one-quarter Egyptian. Another biographer, Michael Grant, makes a convincing case for her having been the daughter of Cleopatra V Tryphaena, the sister and wife of Cleopatra's father, Ptolemy XII Auletes.

We know that Ptolemy XII Auletes was "our" Cleopatra's father, but it has been argued that Cleopatra Tryphaena had been dead for a year by the time Cleopatra VII was born, that Cleopatra Tryphaena was not her mother but her sister, and that Cleopatra VII was the daughter of Ptolemy XII's second wife. The complexities of this intricate and entangled web raise the similarly knotty question of how many siblings Cleopatra had. We are reasonably sure that Ptolemy XII had five children, three daughters and two sons: Berenice IV, Cleopatra VII, Arsinoe IV, Ptolemy XIII, and Ptolemy

XIV. But some have argued for the existence of an older sister, an earlier Cleopatra.

By the terms of her father's will and according to dynastic tradition, she was obliged to run the country with a male consort. The obvious choice was her younger brother Ptolemy XIII, who became her husband and at the time of their ascension to the throne was ten years old. A year before his death, Auletes, who was highly aware of the significance of names and nicknames, and himself had so many, conferred new titles on his heirs: "new gods" and "loving siblings." It was true that the Ptolemaic rulers were worshipped as living deities. But like so many of their Ptolemaic forebears, the sibling-spouses were far from loving, as the world was about to find out.

Cleopatra's problem was not her ten-year-old brother but her brother's advisers. Among them was Pothinus, a court eunuch, who was in charge of the young pharaoh's funds and who had worked to turn the Egyptians against Cleopatra. According to the Roman historian Cassius Dio, Pothinus's fear that his wrongdoings would be discovered inspired him to send for Achillas, a military general "who was still at this time near Pelusium, and by frightening him and at the same time inspiring him with hopes he made him his associate." The third and least powerful of Ptolemy's advisers was Theodotus of Chios, a teacher of rhetoric who was the boy's tutor. "To all of them alike it seemed a shame to be ruled by a woman" (book 42). Together this unlikely triad conspired against a young woman who eventually would prove to be smarter and more resourceful than they were.

In any case, 51 BCE was not the most auspicious moment for a teenager and a child to be crowned queen and king. Egypt's future seemed precarious and unstable. The Romans had long debated annexing the country, but so far the leaders had realized that it was more practical to exploit the nation's riches without stirring up its intermittently restless population. In 65, Marcus Licinius Crassus had suggested to the Roman Senate that Egypt's independence be ended, a proposal that was rejected by the senators, who presumably realized that they could simultaneously exploit Egypt's natural resources and extort fortunes from its beleaguered and desperate leaders.

Rome's appetite for Egypt was not as simple as that of an imperialist aggressor threatening to invade and dismantle an old and intact civilization. It might have looked that way to the Macedonian-Greek Ptolemies after ruling Egypt for three centuries, but they too were descendants of invaders. The threat from Rome was a case in which the leaders of one empire were scheming to replace another, a younger and hungrier world power going up against the remnants of an older one.

By 51, Egypt had lost its holdings in Syria, Palestine, Crete, Cyprus, and the smaller Greek islands. Meanwhile its internal stability had been undermined by a series of rebellions sparked by recurrent famines, corrupt administrators, and the periodic resurgence of ethnic and cultural tensions between the indigenous populations and their Macedonian rulers. The Egyptian coinage had been devalued, and the currency was in free fall. The rates of taxation were unsustainable, and the exorbitant levies were often extorted by force. The land that the peasants worked was the legal property of the pharaoh, who shared some of the profits with rich friends and powerful temple priests.

The Gabiniani—the several thousand soldiers imported by Auletes to fight Berenice—had remained in Egypt and gone rogue, forming criminal gangs, raping women, stealing, terrorizing the country. The population of Alexandria, where the royal family lived, had grown restless and unstable, and the periodic riots had become more violent and frequent.

Meanwhile the most powerful entity in the land—the River Nile, whose annual flooding was at the heart of the country's spiritual life and key to the economic survival of the land that Herodotus called "the gift of the Nile"—seemed to be working against the young queen and her little brother.

In 51 and 50, the floods were disappointing, the consequences frightening.

Drought and famine were constant threats realized all too often throughout Egypt's history. The seven-year Egyptian famine that figures so heavily in the Hebrew Bible has counterparts in myths from around the Middle East.

The Famine Stela, engraved on an enormous block of granite thought to have been inscribed during the reign of Ptolemy VI, tells the story of a seven-year famine that ended after a king prayed to the god who controlled the flooding of the Nile. The final portion of the inscription outlines the sums and sacrifices that people owed the temple in return for the god's intervention: The farmers' entire harvest went to the temple granary. The fishermen and hunters had to surrender a tenth of their catch, and everyone owed the priests 10 percent of their gold, jewels, timber, ochre—whatever they had. The tithing and mass extortion lasted through Cleopatra's reign. She was reluctant to change it, thus losing a major source of revenue and alienating the powerful priests.

The years surrounding Cleopatra's succession were thus lean and troubled ones. In addition to the taxes, the wheat harvests were poor. Widespread hunger led, directly or indirectly, to an outbreak of plague, and food shortages drove starving people from the countryside to the already crowded cities. Rural villages were abandoned, and the priests, left behind, were concerned about the safety of their temples. The crime rate rose along with the prices, and there was a pervasive sense of impending doom and chaos.

On ascending the throne, Cleopatra did everything she could to ameliorate the immediate crisis. Some of her early gestures as queen were largely symbolic but nonetheless significant.

Throughout her reign, she demonstrated her allegiance to the Egyptian gods and goddesses, to Isis and to the animal deities, the hawk- and cat-headed beings that held prominent positions in the Egyptian pantheon. Soon after her coronation, she traveled four hundred miles up the Nile to the temple of Ammon, in Upper Egypt, to assume a visible role in the installation of the Buchis bull, sacred to the god Montu. The Egyptians had worshipped bulls — symbols of power and fertility — from early antiquity. The Apis bull of Memphis, a black bull with white spots, was among the most important Egyptian gods. Herodotus records the (perhaps apocryphal) murder of the Apis bull by the Persian king Cambyses, who conquered Egypt in 525 BCE. The god Serapis, whose worship was promoted by the Ptolemies, incorporated aspects of this bovine deity. But Buchis of Hermonthis, considered to be a vessel for the soul of Amun-ra, was also widely revered.

Conveniently for Cleopatra, the Buchis bull died around the time she came to power, and when a new bull was installed on March 22, 51, Cleopatra thought it politic to attend the ceremony. This event was depicted on the Bucheum Stelae, in an inscription that describes the queen participating in the river procession and transporting the newly consecrated (or about to be consecrated) bull on her royal barge.

From the moment Cleopatra took office, each of her actions and decisions would involve a calculation: weighing the influence of the priests venerated by the same people they oppressed, then factoring in the extent to which religion could secure and extend her power. Though we know nothing of her spiritual life, she clearly understood the importance of demonstrating her fealty to the religion that had remained such a powerful force in Egyptian culture.

She undertook the challenge of stabilizing the currency, adjusting the rates of taxation, fending off her father's debtors, and defusing tensions with Rome. In the process she made mistakes, among them demanding that the wheat produced in the countryside be requisitioned and sent to Alexandria, a decision that, predictably, was popular in the city but deeply resented in the countryside.

Meanwhile she took on the job of curbing the Gabiniani, who not only were wreaking havoc in Egypt but had committed a double murder that without the newly crowned queen's intercession might have progressed into a damaging international incident.

When Marcus Calpurnius Bibulus, the Roman proconsul in Syria, sent his two sons to Egypt, presumably to ask the Gabiniani to help him in his war against the Parthians, the sons were tortured and killed. The murders were thought to have been carried out with the approval of young Ptolemy XIII's advisers Achillas and, most notably, Pothinus, who by then was widely believed to be the true power behind the throne. The Egyptian courtiers were reluctant to lose the services of the private army, and the Gabiniani themselves were apparently less than eager to trade the riotous freedom they were enjoying in Egypt for military service under the Roman governor.

In ordering that the Gabinian murderers be sent to Syria in chains, Cleopatra was attempting not only to solidify her connection with Rome but to rebuke her brother's ambitious and threatening inner circle. Unexpectedly, and not entirely rationally, Bibulus sent the prisoners back, claiming that the right to punish them was a matter best left to the Roman Senate. This was despite the fact that the murders had taken place in Egypt, and that the Gabiniani had more or less cut their ties with Rome and were taking orders from the young pharaoh's advisers.

It had taken great daring for Cleopatra to stand up to the Gabiniani, and her courage made it clear that she intended to rule her country with forcefulness and resolve. It also established a template for the ways in which she would attempt to deal with Rome — more effectively and successfully than her father had.

Her focus on affairs of state, in sharp contrast to her father's rumored preference for his flute, helped build her popularity with at least part of the population. That support would prove invaluable when relations between the queen and her younger brother declined even further over the next three years, gradually and then more drastically after Cleopatra issued a document naming herself the sole ruler of Egypt. It was rumored that from the start she had plotted to kill Ptolemy XIII and replace him with their younger brother, Ptolemy XIV. But like many theories about Cleopatra, there is no evidence to prove it.

For seven years Rome was ruled by Julius Caesar, Pompey, and Crassus, joined in an intermittently tense alliance. In 53, Crassus died fighting the Parthians. The next year saw the death of Julia, Caesar's daughter and Pompey's wife. These events widened the growing division between Caesar and Pompey, the Triumvirate's two remaining members. In 49, a civil war broke out between the forces of Caesar and those of Pompey. Pompey's son Gnaeus Pompeius Magnus traveled to Egypt to secure military and financial aid. At that point, Cleopatra and her brother were ruling in consort, and after Gnaeus Pompeius reminded them of the closeness between his father and theirs — of the loyalty with which Pompey had supported Auletes — they agreed to send Pompey sixty ships, five hundred Gabinian soldiers, and an ample supply of grain. These measures, coming at a time when Egypt was having trouble feeding its own population, could hardly have endeared the monarchs to their subjects.

Around this time, Cleopatra left Alexandria; it is not clear whether she was expelled by her brother (and his advisers) or whether she wisely decided to leave in order to raise an army for the conflict between them that by now must have seemed inevitable. According to Lucan, Pompey had sided with Ptolemy XIII and named the young king as the sole ruler of Egypt.

Together with her younger sister Arsinoe IV, Cleopatra traveled first to Upper Egypt, near Thebes, and then on to Syria in order to prepare for the escalating conflict with the forces, led by the general Achillas, who were fighting to establish her younger brother as the sole monarch.

In 49, Pompey was defeated at the Battle of Pharsalus. Recalling the friendship and aid that Ptolemy XIII and Cleopatra had given him, and hoping to find both refuge and military reinforcements, Pompey fled across the Mediterranean to Egypt. But the young pharaoh's advisers were reluctant to become involved in a Roman war — and especially reluctant to side with their former ally who now seemed all but certain to be the loser.

Writing in the early third century CE, the Roman historian Cassius Dio provides a detailed and rather beautiful account of the murder of Pompey at Pelusium in 48 BCE, where Ptolemy XIII — at that time still only thirteen — was camped in the midst of his war with Cleopatra:

> Bringing the ships to anchor, he sent some men to remind the prince
> of the favour shown his father and to ask that he be permitted to land

under certain definite guarantees; for he did not venture to disembark before obtaining some guarantee of safety. Ptolemy gave him no answer, for he was still a mere boy, but some of the Egyptians . . . came in the guise of friends; but they impiously plotted against him. . . . After many friendly greetings they begged him to come over to their boats, declaring that by reason of its size and the shallow water a ship could not come close to land and that Ptolemy was very eager to see him promptly.

Though the size of the boat dispatched to greet him must have seemed like a bad sign, and though Pompey's men tried to dissuade him from boarding, Pompey trusted the Egyptians and was killed on board the skiff, stabbed from behind even as he held out his hand for help in disembarking. Young Ptolemy XIII is said to have stood by and watched, wearing a purple robe.

[Pompey] uttered not a word and made no complaint, but as soon as he perceived their plot and recognized that he would not be able to ward them off or escape, he veiled his face. . . . Although he had once been, as the saying is, "master of a thousand ships," he was destroyed in a tiny boat near Egypt and in a sense by Ptolemy, whose father he had once restored from exile to that land and to his kingdom.

After the murder, Ptolemy's men beheaded Pompey and tossed his naked corpse into the water, where it remained until one of his men retrieved it and gave it a Roman funeral, cremating it on a modest pyre constructed from a wrecked fishing boat.

If Ptolemy XIII and his advisers believed that killing Pompey was a way to win Caesar's gratitude, they were seriously mistaken. A short time later, Caesar followed Pompey to Egypt, where, according to Plutarch, he mourned the loss of his former friend, ally, and son-in-law. "From the man who brought him Pompey's head he turned away as from a murderer; and when he received Pompey's seal ring, on which was carved a lion holding a sword, he burst into tears."

One can easily imagine the dismay and terror of the thirteen-year-old king, who had witnessed the murder. His advisers' miscalculation not only cost him Caesar's goodwill but would later earn him a special place in Dante's hell, a circle reserved for those guilty of the most wicked betrayals — a place where Ptolemy would spend eternity in the company of Judas Iscariot and Cain. Cassius Dio tells us that Pompey's murderers "brought a curse upon themselves and all Egypt" (book 42).

After pardoning the men who had sided with Pompey and whom his own soldiers had arrested, Caesar stationed himself in a villa on the grounds of the Egyptian royal palace. Outside the gates in Alexandria, fighting had again broken out. Cleopatra and Ptolemy XIII were still battling for control of the country, and Achillas ordered his troops to occupy Alexandria. Caesar attempted to calm the warring nation by brokering a peace accord between Cleopatra and her brother.

This process was made more difficult — and more dangerous — by the interference of the young king's regent, the eunuch Pothinus, who, some said, was planning to murder Caesar just as he had killed Pompey. He enjoyed reminding Caesar and his men of the fortune that Auletes borrowed from Rome, the debt that had been inherited by Ptolemy XIII and that Egypt still owed Rome and was still slow in repaying.

Plutarch tells us that Pothinus had been overheard by Caesar's barber — "an excessively timid fellow, who left nothing uninvestigated, but liked to eavesdrop and meddle" – talking about the plot to kill Caesar. Even in the first century BCE, it seems to have been the case that people have always been inclined to chatter too freely while they are getting their hair cut.

CHAPTER THREE

Caesar and Cleopatra

The story of Cleopatra's initial meeting with Julius Caesar is among the amusing and dramatic anecdotes that Plutarch was unable to resist including in his biography of the Roman leader — a successful calculation, evidenced by the fact that true or not, it has become one of the best-known incidents in the life of Cleopatra.

Plutarch describes how with only one companion, Apollodorus the Sicilian, Cleopatra sailed at dusk in a little boat to the palace at Alexandria, where Caesar was encamped.

It being impossible to escape notice otherwise, she placed herself in a bedding sack and lay at full length, whereupon Apollodorus tied up the sack with a cord and carried it inside to Caesar. We are told that it was by this ingenuity of Cleopatra's that Caesar was first captivated by her, as she showed herself to be a charmer; and so overcome was he by her graciousness and her company that he reconciled her to her brother, Ptolemy, on condition that she rule as Ptolemy's colleague in the kingdom.

Due to a mistranslation, the "bedding sack" was over time transformed into a carpet, perhaps a more pointed expression of the orientalism with which Cleopatra has been viewed. In Jean-Léon Gérôme's 1866 painting *Cleopatra Before Caesar,* the queen has just emerged from what is unmistakably an elaborate Persian rug. She poses languidly, standing with one arm resting on the bare back of the man who has presumably just freed her from the carpet. Her diaphanous gown is cut to expose her breasts and drape fetchingly beneath her belly; her legs are plainly visible beneath the thin cloth, and she gazes across the darkened room at the understandably startled Caesar.

The story of Cleopatra's meeting with Caesar is not entirely implausible. The queen was young, obviously daring, perhaps eager to surprise the older Roman, to charm and fascinate him. The bloodthirstiness of her brother's retinue and the dangers posed by the riots and the ongoing civil war might have made her eager to reach Alexandria and enter Caesar's quarters under cover of darkness, sneaking past her brother's soldiers. Her nation and her life were at stake, so she may well have felt that extreme measures and total secrecy were required.

In an essay dismantling several of the more popular myths about Cleopatra's relationship with Caesar, Erich S. Gruen notes that the bedclothes/rug story appears only in Plutarch and in no other classical source. He considers what we do know—that Caesar requested both siblings to appear before him—and he offers a series of sensible and persuasive observations: "So Cleopatra, if she made an appearance at all, at that point, did not have to arrive surreptitiously in folds of bedding. Indeed, the very idea that the queen of Egypt, claimant to that proud and commanding kingdom, heir to the ancient dynasty of the Ptolemies, and a devotee of formal ceremonies and ritual, would make her initial appearance to Julius Caesar wrapped in a rug is unthinkable."

Was the story about the carpet true, or was it simply how Plutarch — and the generations that followed — wished to imagine the young Cleopatra? Cassius Dio has left us a more restrained, and perhaps more credible, version of the first meeting between Caesar and the Egyptian queen, an account that tells us more about the queen than the stunt she was said to have pulled:

> She sent word to him that she was being betrayed by her friends and asked that she be allowed to plead her case in person. For she was a woman of surpassing beauty, and at that time, when she was in the prime of her youth, she was most striking; she also possessed a most charming voice and a knowledge of how to make herself agreeable to everyone. Being brilliant to look upon and listen to, with the power to subjugate everyone, even a lover-sated man already past his prime, she thought that it would be in keeping with her role to meet Caesar. . . .
> She asked therefore for admission to his presence, and on obtaining permission adorned and beautified herself so as to appear before him in the most majestic and at the same time pity-inspiring guise. When she had perfected her schemes she entered the city (for she had been living outside of it) and by night without Ptolemy's knowledge went into the palace. Caesar, upon seeing her and hearing her speak a few words was forthwith so completely captivated that he at once, before dawn, sent for Ptolemy and tried to reconcile them.

Both Plutarch and Cassius Dio agree that Cleopatra's scheme was based on her having heard that Caesar was something of a libertine, his character "susceptible," notes Dio, "to such an extent that he had his intrigues with ever so many other women — with all, doubtless, who chanced to come his way" (book 42). Wouldn't she have concluded that seducing the Roman leader would hardly require extraordinary theatrics? Suetonius tells us that Caesar "damaged the reputations of a great many women of rank" and quotes a jingle sung by Caesar's soldiers in the Gallic campaign. "Men of Rome, look out for your wives, we're bringing the bald adulterer home."

In his *Pharsalia*, Lucan claims that Cleopatra ("a woman not of our race") traveled to visit Caesar in a little boat and, after bribing the guards to break the chains guarding the harbor, entered the palace unbeknownst to Caesar. Striking about the passage are its overt racism, its lubriciousness, and the ways in which it prefigures representations of Cleopatra by later generations: "That night had fuelled her insolence, the night that first brought a wanton daughter of the Ptolemies to pollute a Roman general's bed. . . . [Caesar] tainted his thoughts with adulterous lust, mixed illicit lovemaking, bastard offspring, with the affairs of war. . . . She would have sought to sway his hard heart in vain, if her beauty had not added to her prayers, and lust pleaded for her. She passed a sinful night with her corrupted arbiter." Lucan describes the decadence and extravagance of Cleopatra's palace, its rafters coated with gold, its walls gleaming with marble, its doors fashioned from ebony inlaid with tortoiseshell and studded with emeralds.

Of the depictions of Cleopatra in literature and on the screen, among the most appalling is the film version of *Caesar and Cleopatra* (1945), adapted from George Bernard Shaw's play and directed by Gabriel Pascal, with Claude Rains and Vivien Leigh in the title roles.

Its portrayal of the palace slaves — naked but for cowrie-shell G-strings, rolling their eyes and waving their arms as they flee in terror from the Roman incursion — is so stunningly racist that it takes a while to recover and register the odiousness of its portrayal of Cleopatra. She is a mindless Egyptian Lolita with a British accent, a flirtatious waif who pops up like a cute little bunny from between the paws of the Sphinx—just in time to meet the much older Caesar, out taking a moonlight stroll in the desert near his camp. Like the Roman leader he is portraying, Rains sports an early version of a comb-over; Caesar was notoriously sensitive about his baldness.

All through their madcap meeting in the desert, Cleopatra fails to recognize her new friend. She has no idea who he is. She explains that she is the Egyptian queen and is terrified of the Roman cannibals, who are arriving to eat them. The female lust for power that so offended Plutarch is not even remotely at issue.

Leigh represents a familiar type from films of the 1940s and 1950s: the irresistible girl child, the naive nymphet who needs an older man to introduce her to her own agency and sexual power. In this case, the older man's concealment of his identity functions as a joke he is playing on the silly girl, the audience, and the Egyptian people. And little Cleopatra never suspects that this kindly, patronizing elderly gentleman is . . . Julius Caesar.

Before World War II, *Pygmalion,* also directed by Pascal, won the Best Adapted Screenplay Oscar and was something of a hit. So presumably that was the story arc (male teacher transforms female diamond-in-the-rough into princess) that the studio was attempting to repeat: Caesar as the imperial Henry Higgins transforming Cleopatra–Eliza Doolittle from a desert urchin into the queen of Egypt, and, despite or because of the significant age gap, falling in love with his prize student.

Caesar's bursts of delight and admiration for his coltish pupil have distressing off-notes. Cleopatra is his "impossible little dream witch," his "divine child." But the grotesqueness of his tutelage is considerably heightened when he schools Cleopatra in the exercise of power by encouraging her to abuse her slaves, first by standing up to her bossy nurse, then by whipping a fleeing Nubian, naked but for his cowrie shells. With Caesar's encouragement, Cleopatra strikes her slave for no reason and in a girlish frenzy that both Caesar and Cleopatra find hilarious and that is supposed to represent a major step toward her learning how to rule a kingdom.

All this leads to the moment when Cleopatra finds out the true identity of her wise older mentor — it's Caesar! — and faints dead away in his lap.

Meanwhile the film offers a disturbing portrait of the boy king Ptolemy XIII as a stupid, surly, androgynous kid. His bloody civil war with Cleopatra is reduced to infantile sibling rivalry, a domestic squabble during which the older sister sticks out her tongue at the younger brother. And there is quite a bit of smirking among the Romans when it is explained that the siblings are also spouses.

The queen-rolled-up-in-the-carpet scene is the centerpiece of the movie. It appears halfway through the film, so the historical timeline (such as it is) has to be significantly altered. As a result, the incident makes even less sense than it does in Plutarch. Cleopatra is not sneaking into her first meeting with Caesar but performing a cute trick designed to keep us engaged at a point when our interest might otherwise be flagging.

Cleopatra's helper, Apollodorus the Sicilian, is a hunky body builder (Stewart Granger) who effortlessly hefts the cocooned queen onto his bare shoulder and slings her partway down his muscular, rippling back. The cocoon in which she is being transported is indeed a Persian carpet, and some part of the ruse involves — inexplicably — her being hoisted up in the air by a derrick. Just when we think things could not be more perverse, the unwrapping of Cleopatra, swathed in several layers of drapery (reminiscent of a mummy) inside the rug, adds a distasteful suggestion of striptease and necrophilia.

Only after surviving the Battle of the Nile by swimming to safety on the back of either Caesar or Apollodorus (it is a bit hard to tell) does the queen come into her own: Caesar has created something of a Frankenstein's monster. She exercises her authority by threatening to flog her harp teacher and throw him into the Nile to be eaten by crocodiles if she plays a wrong note.

One could dismiss this vapid film with its brainless ingenue Cleopatra as the flip side of the coin, the opposite of Cleopatra as the evil seductress. When the subject is a woman, the options are all too familiar: she is either the virgin or the whore. For centuries, the Romans told us she was the latter, but in this film it is more useful for the storyline to make her the ingenue.

Most telling about the film is not only its racism and the frisson of pedophilia but something that Caesar says during that initial meeting in the desert. Still not suspecting that he's one of the cannibal Romans, Cleopatra remarks on his pallor. Caesar replies, "Are you sure it is the moonlight that makes me look whiter than an Egyptian?" That line, underlining the way Cleopatra's alliance with Caesar was seen as an instance of a woman of color entrancing a white man, makes us uncomfortably aware of how much of Cleopatra's story is about imperialism and race. It reminds us that when the film was made, in 1945, British troops were still in Egypt, where they had been since 1882 and where (though the country was by then officially independent) the British Army would remain until 1956. The film's release also preceded by two years Great Britain's departure from India. Despite their togas and comb-overs, these Romans *are* the British, or stand-ins for the British, bringing culture and civilization to the lands they invade, occupy, and exploit. Cleopatra and her fellow Egyptians need the Romans to come in and maintain order. The occupiers will impose their advanced civilization on these primitive who commit incest at the highest societal level. They will *help* the queen govern. And if, in the film, the aging Roman loses his heart to the Egyptian vixen, it makes for a sweeter and more romantic story.

Caesar's attempt to settle the dispute between Cleopatra and her brother could not have begun the way it did in Pascal's version, with the Roman emperor breaking up a family fight, watching with bemused condescension as the sister taunts her brother. By the time Caesar interceded in the sibling power struggle, the bitter and costly rivalry had already begun. Cassius Dio describes the young pharaoh's shock at seeing his sister and Caesar together. Crying out that he was betrayed, he tore the crown from his head and threw it away, provoking his subjects into attacking the palace.

In *The Civil War,* Caesar, writing about himself in the third person, recalls his sense that the war between Cleopatra and her brother "was a matter of concern to the Roman people and to himself." That concern had its roots in the bargain that Rome had reached with Auletes during one of the pharaoh's stays in Rome, and though Caesar fails to mention it, we can assume that his anxiety was not only motivated by his infatuation with Cleopatra, as some have claimed, but was at least in part strategic and financial. Auletes' children were expected to repay the sums that their father had borrowed, and Caesar made it clear that his effort to broker an accord between them was contingent on their promise to honor Auletes' agreement with Rome to repay some part of the 17.5 million drachmas that had been loaned to him.

Predictably unhappy with Caesar's interference, Pothinus mocked this part of the bargain, offering to repay the debt when, and only when, Caesar left Egypt. The notion that Caesar's attempt to mediate the siblings' dispute was motivated by affection for Cleopatra has made for a better story, but one cannot forget how much their history was shaped by concerns of politics and money.

Caesar called an assembly, at which he proclaimed that the establishment of a joint brother-sister monarchy had been their father's intention. As evidence, he produced a copy of Auletes' will, which designated "the elder of his two sons and one of his daughters" as his heirs. Also in the will, Auletes appointed the Roman people as guardians of those heirs, a provision that legitimized Roman interference in Egyptian affairs — yet another unwise and desperate gesture that Auletes had presumably intended to placate and fend off Roman aggression. (Some historians hypothesize that one reason Auletes borrowed so much money was in order to give the Romans a stake in ensuring that he remained in power and was thus able to repay them.)

One wonders why Caesar imagined that the Alexandrians would be swayed by the dying wishes of a king who preferred his flute to his people, who had alienated and impoverished them, and who had ultimately mortgaged them to Rome. Caesar ordered the two warring parties to disband their armies and submit to a legal process that he, as "friend and arbiter," would resolve. Auletes' two younger children, Arsinoe IV and Ptolemy XIV, were made co-rulers of Cyprus, perhaps — given the history of the Ptolemies — to defuse any future threat they might pose to their older siblings' reign.

Once more, driven by ambition and ill will, Ptolemy XIII's guardians undermined any arrangement that failed to put them in complete control. Caesar describes the eunuch Pothinus as being in charge of the kingdom and resentful of Roman interference, while Cassius Dio reasons that Pothinus feared that unless the boy king was declared sole ruler, Pothinus would be made to pay for his bad conduct.

Pothinus sent a secret message to Achillas recalling Ptolemy's army to Alexandria. Hoping to discover Achillas's intention, Caesar dispatched two ambassadors to sound out the general. Achillas had both of them killed, much as Auletes had murdered the Alexandrians sent to meet with him in Rome. It was yet another demonstration of how dangerous it was in antiquity to be an emissary from one hostile faction to another.

Caesar realized that it would be foolish to alienate Ptolemy XIII, who was popular with the Alexandrians. Even when active fighting had broken out and the boy king's army was attacking the Romans, Caesar insisted that the conflict was not the work of Ptolemy but of his rogue advisers, an assertion that was probably true, given the boy's age and lack of political experience. The character and quality of Achillas's army was of little interest to Plutarch but of great concern to Caesar. He reports on the unsavory character of the troops from backgrounds that, he suggests, might make them at once disorganized and especially ferocious.

The army he describes was composed of the Gabiniani, who had remained in Egypt after defending Auletes against his daughter. Ill-disciplined and removed from the "orderly conduct" of Roman soldiers, these exiles, former citizens of the empire, criminals, and runaway slaves, had little regard for the higher ideals and principles of the Roman military: "By a long-established custom of the Alexandrian army, these men habitually demanded that friends of the king be put to death, plundered the property of the rich, laid siege to the king's residence to win higher pay, and removed some and appointed others to the throne."

Ultimately, the moral character of the Egyptian soldiers mattered less than the fact that Caesar's forces were greatly outnumbered. Fighting broke out in the streets of Alexandria, and Achillas seized control of the city, except in the district where Caesar had taken refuge in the royal palace. Achillas attempted to break into the royal compound, but Caesar's men, tactically deployed in the streets of Alexandria, thwarted the assault. The most serious fighting took place in the harbor; it was clear that whoever seized control of the port would probably win the war. Caesar ordered that his own ships be burned to prevent the enemy from gaining control of them; in the ensuing chaos, he was able to seize control of the lighthouse (the Pharos) and the narrow waterway that controlled access to the port.

The fighting lasted all through the fall of 48 BCE. In most ways Plutarch's account follows Caesar's, though he suggests—and quickly glosses over—that the burning of the fleet resulted in the destruction of the library of Alexandria after the flames were blown to shore. He adds that Caesar, forced to swim to safety, held a number of manuscripts in his hand. "Though he was continually darted at, and forced to keep his head often under water, yet he did not let go, but held them up, safe from wetting in one hand, whilst he swam with the other." (Caesar was famous for his expert swimming.)

Were they scrolls rescued from the burning library or, more likely, manuscripts of his own writings? Caesar's preservation of the manuscripts is one of those memorable and convincing details, like Pompey's funeral pyre having been built from the wrecked boat.

And so the ruin or partial ruin of a miraculous collection became a story about a superhero who knew the value of the written word.

Over the intervening years, there has been considerable debate about how much of the library was burned and how the fire started. One theory suggests that Caesar accidentally ignited the blaze when he ordered his own ships burned in the harbor to prevent Achillas's army from using them against the Romans. Others have cited a later date for the damage to the collection and blamed the Roman emperor Theodosius and the Muslim caliph Omar. The library seems to have existed when Strabo visited Alexandria in 24 CE, and Suetonius tells us that it survived well into the first century CE, when a new wing was added to contain the massive number of books written by the emperor Claudius.

But it also seems that the library's decline may have begun much earlier, when Ptolemy VII replaced the librarian, a Homeric scholar, with his crony, a military man. As Duane Roller notes, "Filling senior administrative posts with ideologues is clear evidence of the kingdom's decline. This pattern seems to have continued into the next generation, when Ptolemy also appointed a confidant as Librarian." It is also possible that the library was not destroyed suddenly by fire but deteriorated slowly over time, damaged by the elements and a series of natural disasters.

As the war continued, a secondary power struggle broke out when Cleopatra's sister and former ally, Arsinoe, went over to the side of her brother, then quarreled with Achillas and was forced to resort to bribing their soldiers to retain their support. Though Pothinus continued to exhort Achillas to prolong the fighting, his messengers were arrested, and Pothinus was put to death. The story of Caesar's barber and the overheard plot to poison the emperor does not appear in Caesar's account, which is more concerned with military and political problems and solutions than with gossip.

The author of *The Alexandrian War*—believed to be Aulus Hirtius, a military subordinate of Caesar's who rose (briefly) to the position of consul after the emperor's death—is, like Caesar, focused on strategy when he describes how the city was fortified after Arsinoe ordered that Achillas be killed. For Arsinoe had by then declared herself queen and replaced the leader of her brother's army with her tutor, the eunuch Ganymedes, who persuaded her that Achillas was planning to betray the fleet and should therefore be punished.

Meanwhile a revolutionary fervor was arising in the Egyptian capital in the midst of the war. Alexandria's leaders reminded their people of how long they had been fending off Rome's incursions and warned that if Caesar were permitted to remain among them their kingdom would be reduced to a Roman province.

Through an elaborate feat of military engineering, Ganymedes cut off the water supply to the neighborhood in which Caesar was staying, enraging Caesar's Alexandrian neighbors. And now Hirtius's narrative breaks into the uncharacteristic first person as, presumably speaking for his commander, he rails against the people with whom Caesar was at war. "If I had to defend the Alexandrians against the charges of deceitfulness and opportunism, I could speak for a long time to no purpose; indeed, the moment you recognize their race you also recognize their character, and no one can doubt that this is a people made for treachery."

Reading these lines, one may think of Claude Rains, preening in the moonlight, asking if the pale moon glow was really the only reason he looked whiter than the Egyptians. In the phrase "a people made for treachery," we hear the imperialist accepting his sacred duty to bring civilization and morality to a population. Hirtius is speaking in the voice of a Roman leader who within a few years would be brutally assassinated by his own people on the floor of the Senate.

Even as Caesar was ordering his men to dig wells and find fresh water, reinforcements arrived to shore up the Egyptian army, though not enough to resist the brilliant deployment of the Roman naval forces mustered in an effort to intimidate their opponents. More fighting followed, further attacks and retreats, until the Alexandrians, who had believed that they were (in Hirtius's words) "our equals" were disheartened and demoralized.

Impressed by the Romans' resolve and military acumen, the Alexandrians came to Caesar and asked him to release Ptolemy from Roman custody and in the process to deliver them from Arsinoe and the tyrannical Ganymedes.

Arsinoe was exiled to Ephesus, a decision for which Aulus Hirtius credits Caesar. ("He decided to remove from the kingdom the younger girl, Arsinoe.") The most famous painting of Cleopatra's younger sister is Tintoretto's ca. 1560 *The Deliverance of Arsinoe*. It purports to show Arsinoe's escape from Alexandria after Caesar helped her sister gain control of Egypt. Two men and two women in a boat are about to head out onto the roiling ocean. Both women have beautiful bodies and are naked but for some heavy, strategically draped chains. We are not intended to wonder why they would have decided to take this dangerous sea voyage naked, or why the woman in the soldier's arms is supposed to be the Egyptian princess who attempted to steal her sister's throne.

The later killing of her younger sister in 41 BCE is one of the sibling murders that Cleopatra is considered to have ordered, and to have asked Mark Antony to carry out for her. Arsinoe was purportedly dragged out of the Temple of Artemis at Ephesus and slaughtered on its steps.

Tiring of the costly war and distressed by the growing number of casualties, the Alexandrians promised to surrender if Caesar came to their aid, a request that inspires yet another tirade from Aulus Hirtius about the deceitful people, "always keeping one aim in view and pretending to another."

Still attempting to arrange a peaceful settlement, Caesar prevailed upon Ptolemy to think of his country and his people. In tears, the young pharaoh agreed, and Caesar released him, although he had no faith in the young pharaoh, because of his youth and his lack of education. "Then the king, like a racehorse given his head, started to wage war against Caesar with such energy that the tears he had shed when talking to Caesar were obviously tears of joy." Ptolemy drowned in the midst of the fighting: "It is generally agreed that the king himself got away from the camp, and was taken on board ship, but died when the ship sank under the numbers of men who swam out to the nearest vessels."

Cleopatra is notably absent from these accounts, suggesting that she remained in the royal palace and waited to see how the conflict would be resolved.

The young Ptolemy's death brought an end to the civil war. The Egyptian army surrendered. Greeted as a hero and a victor, Caesar accepted the Alexandrians' defeat and celebrated with his men. "Now that he was in control of Egypt and Alexandria, Caesar established on the throne the monarchs whom Ptolemy had appointed in his will and bound the Roman people by oath to see were not altered. Since the elder of the two boys, who had been king, was no more, Caesar gave the throne to the younger boy [Ptolemy XIV] and to Cleopatra, the elder of the two daughters, who had remained loyal to him."

Cleopatra, the elder of the two daughters, who had remained loyal to him. And that's it. Nowhere in either *The Civil War* or *The Alexandrian War* does Caesar or Hirtius mention the emperor's romance with Cleopatra; nowhere do they refer to his being trapped in her palace; nowhere do they raise the possibility that the burning of his fleet led to the destruction of the great library; nowhere do they acknowledge the celebratory voyage along the Nile that Caesar and Cleopatra were said to have taken.

Nor does either of these authors write anything to suggest that the Egyptian queen has had, or would have, Caesar's child. This view of their relationship and of the power balance between them would lead the historian Ronald Syme to conclude, "Cleopatra was of no moment whatsoever in the policy of Caesar the Dictator" (quoted in Roller).

Plutarch tells a different story: a version of events that supports his case against Cleopatra for interfering in the affairs of Rome and that at the same time makes Caesar seem even more heroic than he appears in his own account.

Though Caesar reports that his military intervention in Egypt was inspired purely by the desire to broker a peace and persuade a brother and sister to share the throne, Plutarch insists that he would never have gotten involved in the Alexandrian war if not for his infatuation with Cleopatra, although, Plutarch also suggests, it was possible that he was enraged by Pothinus's plotting against him, by the eunuch's arrogance, and by the insults — most of them concerning the fortunes that Pothinus accused Caesar of stealing from Egypt — leveled against the emperor and his soldiers.

Cassius Dio also acknowledges the central role played by Caesar's affection for Cleopatra, suggesting that Caesar's reluctance to claim Egypt for Rome was a consequence of his fondness for the Egyptian queen, "for whose sake he had waged the conflict." But because of his fear that the Egyptians might rebel again if a woman assumed control of the country, "he commanded her to 'marry' her other brother, and gave the kingdom to both of them, at least nominally. For in reality Cleopatra was to hold all the power alone, since her husband was still a boy, and in view of Caesar's favor, there was nothing that she could not do. Hence her living with her brother and sharing rule with him was a mere pretence which she accepted, whereas in truth she ruled alone and spent her time in Caesar's company" (book 42).

Yet another detail, missing from *The Civil War* and *The Alexandrian War,* appears in Plutarch's brief aftermath to the Roman victory: "Leaving Cleopatra reigning in Egypt—she soon bore him a son, whom the Alexandrians called Caesarion." An inscription on the Serapeum in Memphis suggests that Caesarion was born near the end of June 47.

Caesar and Cleopatra are said—though this too has been disputed—to have celebrated their victory in the spring of 47 with a cruise along the Nile, accompanied by a fleet of four hundred ships. Writes Suetonius, "With her too, he journeyed by royal barge deep into Egypt, and would have reached Ethiopia but his army refused to follow him." Allegedly the flotilla also included a royal barge as spacious, luxuriously furnished, and comfortable as a floating villa.

However, early in that same spring, after approving plans for a temple dedicated to him, Caesar left Egypt for Anatolia, where an anti-Roman insurrection had broken out. He seems not to have been present in Alexandria that June, when Caesarion—officially, Ptolemy Philopator Philometor Caesar—was born. Suetonius again: "The child born to her he allowed to be called by his name. Indeed, several Greek writers record that he was like Caesar in both appearance and bearing. Mark Antony confirmed to the senate that Caesar had actually acknowledged the child . . . and others of Caesar's friends were aware of this." This claim was disputed by Gaius Oppius, who published a book asserting that Caesarion was not Caesar's child. And despite what Suetonius wrote, it seems clear that Caesar never publicly acknowledged Caesarion's paternity.

Allegedly in love with Cleopatra even before their affair began,

Antony was later said to have been smitten by his first sight of her when she was a girl. He would have had a compelling reason to support the claim that her son was Caesar's heir—a fact that she spent much time and effort attempting to establish. Antony's own fate might have turned out differently had his lover's son, instead of Caesar's grandnephew Octavian, been designated by Julius Caesar to rule the Roman Empire after his death. In any case, Caesar chose Octavian as his heir, a decision that would have serious, indeed fatal, consequences for both Antony and Cleopatra.

After Caesar's departure, Cleopatra was left with the task of repairing the damage that the war had inflicted on Alexandria. The gymnasium that so impressed Strabo was reconstructed, as was the lighthouse on the island of Pharos, a landmark that had not only a practical purpose but a highly symbolic significance in the life of the city. She also initiated the building of a large complex, the Caesareum, dedicated to Julius Caesar, and of her own tomb, appropriately located near the Temple of Isis. This crypt, allegedly impossible to open once it had been closed, would factor heavily in the story of her death and that of Antony, as well as in the works of art and literature that these events inspired.

In addition to all her civic projects and responsibilities, Cleopatra was also the mother of four children: a son with Julius Caesar and fraternal twins (a girl and a boy) and another son with Mark Antony. Given the ready availability of contraception and abortion, skills and techniques at which the Egyptian doctors were said to be adept, it seems likely that these were children she wanted. By luck or design, their arrivals were evenly spaced, giving the queen ample time to recover from the strains of pregnancy and childbirth, physical demands that would have compromised her ability to function at full capacity and strength. Though the war against her brother had eliminated one threat to her power, it would still have seemed unwise to relax her vigilance for an extended period of time.

We have already seen how twisted, frayed, and easily severed family bonds were among the Ptolemies. Having children with powerful men was no guarantee of safety, as it might be today. Cleopatra not only protected her children but fought for them. With her family history and Egypt's unstable position, she might well have suspected that their survival depended on hers, and that she could not safely assume her children would outlive her.

That she appears to have lobbied Caesar to acknowledge their son as his heir and successor reveals her maternal passions combined with her own ambition. Since Caesarion was just a baby, and since (despite his heroic swim) Caesar was known to be aging and in declining health, the emperor's death and the installation of Caesar and Cleopatra's son in his place would have meant that Cleopatra acted as regent for Caesarion—and controlled not only Egypt but the entire Roman Empire. After Caesar's assassination and the death of her last remaining brother, Ptolemy XIV, Cleopatra had Caesarion appointed as her co-ruler.

Later, after his mother's death, Caesarion, then just thirteen, was executed by Octavian. He had been smuggled out of Egypt, but Octavian tricked him into returning. The other three children were taken to Rome and given over to the care of Octavian's sister, Octavia the Younger, Antony's former wife, with whom Antony had had two children.

In 46, the year after her son's birth, Cleopatra traveled to Rome and stayed in Caesar's Trastevere villa, where Caesar gave her the run of his luxurious house and lush gardens. These were located near where the Villa Farnesina—now a museum with magnificent wall paintings by Raphael, del Piombo, and others — stands today. The Villa Farnesina was constructed in the early sixteenth century, but we can assume that the banker, Agostino Chigi, who built it recognized, as did Caesar, an especially beautiful spot. Located on the west bank of the Tiber, across the river and some distance from the Forum, it would have helped Caesar keep Cleopatra away from the disapproving eyes of the senators. The Renaissance villa that stands on the site of the ancient one occupies a lovely strip of flat land (now bisected by a somewhat sooty stretch of the via della Lungara) abutting the jungly greenery of the Janiculum Hill that rises above it.

Officially, the queen's visit signified a formal attempt to recognize and strengthen the treaties that her father had forged, at such great financial cost, with Rome. It is not known whether Cleopatra brought Caesarion with her. If her real mission was to have Caesar recognize his son, bringing the baby along might or might not have made this more likely.

Arranging for the empire to be passed down through the Ptolemaic line would have been extremely unpopular with the Romans, who already disapproved of Cleopatra's presence in the capital and of her unashamedly public relationship with Caesar. Given the status of Roman women, who were wholly subservient to their male guardians, the simple fact of Cleopatra's existence would have seemed to the men of Rome a provocation and an affront. Nor would they have been much reassured when during that period, or at some time before, a gold-plated statue of Cleopatra was installed in the temple of Venus Genetrix, in the Forum.

Cassius Dio remarks on the Romans' disapproval of Caesar's relationship with Cleopatra, an affair that had only been rumored when the Egyptian queen was in Alexandria, but which was impossible to ignore once she had come to Rome. "For she had come to the city with her husband and settled in Caesar's own house, so that he too derived an ill repute on account of both of them. He was not at all concerned, however, about this" (book 43).

Among Cleopatra's most bitter and influential enemies was Cicero, the powerful orator, who was nearing sixty and had recently divorced his wife to marry his young ward. In a letter to Atticus, dated June 13, 44, he wrote, "I can't stand the queen." Cleopatra seems to have promised Cicero something—a book, it is thought, or possibly a manuscript—that she failed to deliver, and she insulted him again when she sent an emissary to Cicero's house asking not for an audience with Cicero but to see his friend Atticus. His rancor had not yet dissipated two years later when he wrote to Atticus: "The queen's insolence, too, when she was living in Caesar's trans-Tiberine villa, I cannot recall without a pang." Perhaps Cleopatra failed to appreciate or honor the extent of the orator's political clout. But with her skills as a diplomat and her necessary sensitivity to power relations, it seems probable that she knew what she was doing and was testing Caesar's loyalties and possibly having fun at Cicero's expense. Cicero's hatred for Cleopatra and Antony survived Caesar's death. His bitter quarrel with Antony would lead to his own fatal and gory fall from grace.

In any case, the problem with Cleopatra's presence in Trastevere was not so much the scandalous love affair with Caesar or her slighting of Cicero but the threat that she (and the possible succession of her son) was perceived to pose to the empire—as well as the high cost of her maintenance, which the Romans were financing. According to Suetonius, Caesar refused to let his Egyptian lover depart until he had "showered her with the greatest honours and gifts." And by the time she left Rome, she had been officially recognized as an "allied monarch."

It is unclear how much of her visit Cleopatra spent in Rome. It has been suggested that she remained for two years, but it seems unlikely that she would have spent so long away from the nation for which she had fought so hard, a country that was difficult to rule in normal times, and even more so in periods of drought and economic hardship. Doubtless she would have learned from observing the consequences of her father's bad decisions about the damage incurred by a leader who lingered too long in another country, enjoying a potential enemy's hospitality, and trying to bribe or cajole foreign leaders and turn aggressors into allies.

Another problem that would have militated against Cleopatra's extended absence was the fact that her younger sister Arsinoe had not given up on her plans to usurp the Egyptian throne. Exiled to Ephesus, Arsinoe again set about gathering support—and again declared herself queen of Egypt.

We know that Cleopatra was in Rome on the Ides of March, 44.

No matter how often we hear it, the story of Julius Caesar's assassination never loses its power to fascinate and shock us. For this we can thank the early chroniclers, who singled out among the events and rumors details and plot turns to give us narratives that demonstrate what brilliant writers these classical authors were.

Suetonius—always so fascinated by omens—starts up the drumbeat with a passage about the portents that Caesar ignored, how Caesar remained unfazed when he fell down while disembarking from a ship or when a sacrificial victim escaped before the ceremony could be performed. (Plutarch chooses a more lurid incident, or perhaps a more sensational version of the same one: in midsacrifice, Caesar discovered that the victim's heart was missing.) Fond of tabulating the balance of virtue and vice, Suetonius praises Caesar's generosity, fairness, unselfishness, and bravery, and his "astonishing moderation and mercy," and offers examples of good behavior illustrating each of his strengths. According to Suetonius, Caesar excelled as a city planner, a government reformer, a long-distance horseback rider, and a lucid and eloquent writer.

After that, the bad news: "Other things he did and said outweighed these, so that it is thought he abused his power and was justly killed." Suetonius compiles a list of those other things: the arrogance, the snubs, the insults, the ruthless and destabilizing ambition. Presumably, the Romans knew their leader's weaknesses and strengths, but, as frequently happens in political life, a proliferation of damning rumors made the Roman senators begin to revise their view of—and fears about—Caesar.

Cleopatra's presence was certainly unhelpful. It may have been seen as confirming the widespread suspicion that Caesar was planning to move to Alexandria and take the riches of the empire with him, though one might sensibly have wondered why Caesar would relocate to a country where he was disliked and whose citizens he had barely pacified in the aftermath of a bitter civil war.

The rumors about Caesar leaving his debt-ridden capital, abandoning a society burdened by the expenses of conducting so many foreign wars, and decamping for Egypt would have been stoked by the fact that Cleopatra, her brother-king, and their retinue were living in his villa. Her presence tapped into a rich vein of unfriendly gossip. It is one thing to believe that your leader has been bewitched by a wicked seductress, quite another to imagine that he is going to leave you for her. The suspicions about Cleopatra's intentions would outlive them both, tainting Plutarch's view of her and those of later writers who took their cue from him.

The most damning and indeed fatal rumor was that Caesar, who had already declared himself dictator for life, now planned to be crowned king, a direct challenge to the foundational principles of the Roman republic. And so, to avoid being forced to accept the rumored coronation, Caesar's would-be assassins and a larger co-hort of co-conspirators decided to accelerate their plan.

First came more chilling portents: Workmen uncovered an ancient tomb with ominous inscriptions. On the night before the Ides of March, Caesar and his wife, Calpurnia, both had nightmares. She dreamed that the pediments of their house collapsed. The couple was awoken when their bedroom door blew open. A herd of horses that had been instrumental in Caesar's crossing the Rubicon was said to be refusing to eat and weeping copiously. Caesar's inconsolable horses is another of those marvelous details that stay with us, telescoping the distance between antiquity and the present.

These were the sort of omens that Romans ignored at their peril. But Caesar paid no attention. His wife begged him to stay at home, but he refused and went to the Senate.

Suetonius describes Caesar's shock, the twenty-three stab wounds, and his effort to wrap his toga around himself so that he would be more decent when he fell, a detail that echoes several accounts of the death of Pompey's murder by the agents of Cleopatra's brother. We read about Caesar's single groan, his astonishment at Brutus's involvement. The funeral orations, the pyre, the public grief. The speculation that Caesar, aware that he was aging, had been ready for death and expressed a preference for a sudden and unexpected end.

He had designated as his heir his grandnephew Gaius Octavius—later Octavian, later still the emperor Augustus. This ended Cleopatra's hope that she could continue to rule Egypt and inherit the empire through her son with Caesar, Caesarion.

Plutarch's depiction of the murder and its aftermath is several times longer, more detailed, and more violent than that of Suetonius, and it is a stellar example of dramatic narrative. A comparison of the two versions offers a clear demonstration of how different writers tell the same story. In Plutarch, the monitory doors and windows in Caesar's house all blow open at the same moment. The violence of the murder is so terrifying and eloquently described that though Plutarch lived long after Caesar, he produced what seems like an eyewitness account that we read with growing horror.

"When Caesar entered the chamber, the Senate rose out of respect." A few assassins stood behind him, pretending to have requests, which Caesar angrily dismissed. Then, "Tillius grabbed his toga with both hands and pulled it down from his neck, which was the signal for the assault. Casca gave him the first blow with his dagger, in the neck, inflicting a wound that was not mortal, nor even deep, as was likely coming from one who at the beginning of such a momentous exploit was unnerved. Caesar instantly turned about, grabbed hold of the dagger, and held it fast." Some senators were appalled, "but each of those who had prepared for the murder bared his dagger and surrounded Caesar. Whichever way he turned he met with blows aimed at his face and eyes, and was driven here and there like a wild beast, trapped in everyone's hands. For all had to begin the sacrifice and taste of the murder, which is why Brutus also stabbed him in the groin. It is said by some that he fought against all the rest, shifting his body this way and that and crying out, but that when he saw Brutus with his drawn sword he covered his head with his toga and let himself fall, either by chance or pushed there by his murderers, at the base of the pedestal on which Pompey's statue stood. The slaughter drenched it with blood, so that Pompey himself seemed to have presided over the vengeance wrought upon his enemy, who lay at his feet, quivering from a multitude of wounds. For he is said to have received twenty-three. And many of the conspirators were wounded by one another as they strove to land their blows in one body."

Plutarch too reminds us of Caesar's stated preference for an "unexpected death," But neither he nor Suetonius remarks on the fact that when someone wishes for a quick and unexpected death, they generally mean a sudden collapse, the body's unforeseen betrayal, or, at worst, an accident, an injury in battle — not being stabbed twenty-three times on the floor of the Senate.

Nowhere in Plutarch's account of the killing is Cleopatra mentioned. But for us it has become an important element in the story. On the day of the murder, Cleopatra was in Rome as the guest of Caesar, her lover, political ally, and defender — and the father of her child.

Perhaps the most believable cinematic portrayal of what the Forum must have been like in the time of Caesar and during the period of Cleopatra's sojourn in Rome is, paradoxically, among the most modern. Paolo and Vittorio Taviani's 2012 film *Caesar Must Die* documents the rehearsals and performance of Shakespeare's *Julius Caesar* in the Rebibbia jail in the suburbs of Rome. The actors are all prisoners. Watching it, we realize that these brooding, rough-edged criminals, some in jail for major crimes, are closer to what the ancient Romans must have been like than the performers who have subsequently portrayed them: Marlon Brando, James Mason, John Gielgud. The performers in the Taviani film are so raw, so intense, taking the story so seriously and with so much at stake that they remind us that what happened on the floor of the Senate was a matter of life and death.

These murderers playing murderers planning a murder give us a different sense of how the scene played out on that Ides of March. Once you have seen the film, your thinking about those senators will have shifted from Shakespeare's eloquent conspirators to a bunch of hardened toughs executing antiquity's version of a gangland-style hit.

"Of the murderers," writes Suetonius, "virtually none of them survived more than three years or met a natural end. All were condemned, each meeting a different fate, some by shipwreck, others in battle. A few even took their own lives with the same dagger that had been used to make their impious attack on Caesar." Plutarch elaborates: "The most remarkable of human coincidences was that which befell Cassius, who . . . killed himself with the same dagger he had used against Caesar. Among the divine signs, there was the great comet, which shone brilliantly for seven nights after Caesar's murder and then disappeared, and the dimness of the sun. For during that year the disc rose pale and without brightness, and the heat it gave off was feeble and meager. The air, accordingly, was dark and heavy . . . and the fruits, imperfect and half-ripened, withered and shriveled from the cold."

But before any real order had been imposed on the chaos that followed Caesar's murder, Cleopatra would be involved in the alliances and antagonisms that pitted his supporters against his enemies. Once again, the battles that set Romans against Romans would have profound repercussions for the Egyptian queen.

Anyone who has lived through any of the disasters of the past half-century—the earthquakes, plagues, and tsunamis; 9/11; the assassinations of Martin Luther King and President Kennedy; the 2021 assault on the U.S. Capitol—will have a vivid sense of what it is like to breathe the air of violence and crisis, how it feels to live in a city in chaos, a world in which a cataclysm has occurred.

After Caesar's assassination, his last will and testament was read aloud to the Roman people, who learned that each of them had received "a generous bequest." This, it seems, was the tipping point. The crowd exploded. They heaped up the available wooden furniture in the Forum to make a funeral pyre for Caesar, then rampaged through the streets, seeking revenge on his killers, all of whom had the good sense to go into hiding.

Cleopatra found herself in a foreign country with her child, or separated from him, after the murder of the man who was not only her lover and the child's father but a vital source of personal, political, and economic support. He was the principal reason that she was in Rome. The rioting and chaos would surely have reminded her of how far from home she was and how little the Romans liked her.

In the turmoil that followed the murder, even Caesar's friends wondered how much danger they were in. Mark Antony, who had not participated in the attack, went into hiding and emerged wearing armor beneath his tunic.

Before we worry too much about Cleopatra, we need to recall that she was no stranger to violence. She had waged a bloody, expensive war with her brother, endured a siege, watched her harbor burn — and emerged the victor. She belonged to a royal dynasty for whom assassination was a far more common way to leave the world than natural death.

Even so, the final days of her Roman sojourn must have been frightening. Cleopatra remained in the city for another few weeks, in the weak cold light and beneath the brilliance of the comet that blazed each night, a phenomenon that was believed to be a reminder of — and a heavenly reproach for — the killing.

Of course, Cleopatra was never directly implicated in the death of Caesar, as she would be later in that of Mark Antony. Her presence in Rome — indeed her very existence — had fueled the distrust and suspicion of Caesar's detractors. But people knew who the conspirators were, and she was not among them, nor would she have had reason to be.

Caesar and Cleopatra

———

A month after Julius Caesar's death, Cleopatra returned to Egypt, which had remained relatively tranquil in her absence, untroubled by the civil disturbances that had blighted so much of her father's and her own early reign. She took advantage of the peaceful and prosperous moment to resume the construction projects that the earlier Ptolemies had begun. She continued work on the massive temple at Dendera, where she had a bas-relief of Caesarion carved into the wall. The image of her son making an offering to Isis underlined the connection between his mother and the Egyptian goddess. Around the same time, Cleopatra ordered the completion of the temple at Edfu, and added to the temple at Hermonthis, where in 51, at the start of her reign, she had installed the sacred bull.

Surrounding herself with prominent philosophers, scientists, and writers, she endeavored to regenerate the intellectual and artistic life of Alexandria, restoring it to something close to what it had been during the reigns of Ptolemy I and II. She herself was said to be the author of treatises on cosmetics, alchemy, and medicine. By the end of her reign, her country had recovered from the economic crisis precipitated by her father's indebtedness, to the extent that eventually she was able to finance and support Antony's military campaigns.

She accomplished all this despite an additional series of disasters that might have tested, and defeated, a less clever and confident ruler. In the spring of 43, and again in the following year, the Nile failed to spill over its banks, resulting in yet another severe drought and famine, as well as an outbreak of plague. By now Cleopatra had more experience than she had had in 51, when she had requisitioned the wheat for the capital. This time she distributed free wheat to her hungry population, curbed the power of the tax collectors, and devalued the currency.

Her brother-husband-consort Ptolemy XIV died around this time, at the age of fifteen. If it is true that Cleopatra had her youngest brother killed so that Caesarion would inherit the Egyptian throne, there were no witnesses, no firsthand accounts, no evidence; we have no idea what happened to the teenage pharaoh. His sister may have poisoned him, or the story of his death may have been yet another expression of what history thought—and expected— of Cleopatra.

Whatever its cause, his death could hardly have been more timely. Cleopatra took the opportunity to have Caesarion declared pharaoh.

In many ways, these were the most productive, and certainly the least troubled, years of Cleopatra's reign, though she faced yet another set of challenges resulting from the ongoing strife among Caesar's surviving assassins and those determined to avenge him. Cleopatra gave military and naval assistance to Dolabella, one of Caesar's allies, who seems to have promised that Caesarion would be chosen as the ruler of Rome. But Cassius intercepted and seized the ships meant for Dolabella, who committed suicide after he was defeated in 43. Though Cleopatra attempted to send more ships enabling Antony and Octavian to fight against Cassius, her efforts were undermined by storms at sea.

In an attempt to determine Cleopatra's true loyalties, and perhaps to reprimand her for her failure to more vigorously support the allies of her dead lover and the father of her son, an emissary— the disloyal and opportunistic Quintus Dellius—arrived to arrange a meeting between Cleopatra and Antony, a meeting that would dramatically change the course of Cleopatra's life.

CHAPTER FOUR

Mark Antony

And so we approach the moment when Plutarch's attention turns to Cleopatra, who so fully engaged his interest that, as is often said, she hijacked his *Life of Antony*. Though this is a bit of a stretch, Plutarch's treatment of Cleopatra has something in common with Tolstoy's portrayal of Anna Karenina. That is, we can watch both writers becoming fascinated, admiring, even a little in love with the woman they set out to condemn for her wayward-ness and depravity.

Plutarch describes the generous and noble household in which Antony was raised, a family idyll interrupted when Antony's step-father was put to death by Cicero for taking part in a conspiracy, an event that inspired Antony's lifelong hatred of Cicero — and that contributed to the joy that Antony would have when he had the orator executed.

Soon enough, Antony's good character succumbed to the cor-rupting influences of his friends, first Gaius Scribonius Curio, and then Publius Clodius Pulcher. In Plutarch's telling, Clodius seems to have been something of a rogue and a sociopath. Clodius's exploits included dressing as a woman to sneak in to see Caesar's wife, Pompeia, with whom he was in love, and who was celebrating a sacred rite that only women were permitted to witness. Later, Antony would marry Clodius's widow, Fulvia — the woman, Plutarch jokes, whom Cleopatra should have paid tuition for teaching Antony to obey a woman.

Egypt enters Antony's history early on, when he supports Cleopatra's father in his bid for Roman aid. He was the one who persuaded Gabinius — founder of the army that later terrorized Alexandria — to invade Egypt and restore Ptolemy XII to the throne that Berenice had seized. Antony soon distinguished himself as a military commander and strategist, leading his army through deep sands and sodden marshes, then across a narrow pass to defeat Berenice's army at Pelusium. He was not only victorious but merciful, a true Roman hero. He dissuaded the enraged Ptolemy from executing the rebel soldiers. This is a recurring theme in Plutarch: the Roman soldier's compassion for the vanquished versus the "less civilized" *Eastern* thirst for enemy blood; it is yet another example of the imperialist myth of cultural, religious, and moral superiority.

Though it is impossible to imagine what Cleopatra knew, it seems unlikely that an intelligent teenager would not have understood that Mark Antony — who, Plutarch claims, Cleopatra met as a girl — had helped save her father and her kingdom. Plutarch tells us that Antony left Alexandria having won the respect of both the Alexandrians and the Roman soldiers.

Plutarch admires Antony, at least at first — before he began taking orders from a woman. He was handsome, a stylish dresser. Plutarch cannot list his worst qualities — he is boastful, loud, badly behaved — without adding in the same sentence that these traits were part of what made him popular. Antony was beloved of his men, relaxed and forgiving on the subject of love affairs, both his own and other people's.

But Antony had a fatal flaw. He was, Plutarch tells us, excessively susceptible to the bad influence of others, and so we are prepared for the destructive effects of the woman who will be in Plutarch's view the worst influence of all.

When Antony failed to broker an agreement between the supporters of Caesar and Pompey, he disguised himself as a servant to bring Caesar the bad news. (This was the first of several times that Antony put on the costume and manners of the lower classes, sometimes because it seemed safer and more expedient, and sometimes for his own amusement.) Antony and Cicero had not stopped despising each other, and Cicero blamed Antony for inciting the civil war between Pompey and Caesar, comparing him to Helen of Troy (another instigator of conflict): how invidious it must have been for a Roman to be compared to a woman, even a mythical beauty. Writing a century later, Plutarch disagrees with Cicero: Caesar would never have attacked Pompey because he got a bad report from Antony. Rather, Caesar was moved by what has always motivated conquerors, the love of power and the "desire to be first and greatest."

When Caesar left Rome to fight Pompey in Spain, he appointed Antony tribune, a role in which Antony managed to lower his standing with the Roman people. The prevailing opinion was that he was overly free with his men, too lazy and preoccupied with pleasure to listen to complainants and petitioners, and given to sleeping with other men's wives. But his brilliance as a military strategist helped Caesar win a series of battles, culminating in the decisive Battle of Pharsalus, where Antony played a major role in Pompey's defeat.

Back in Rome, Antony became even more unpopular. The Romans despised his drunkenness, his reckless spending, his love affairs, "his days spent in sleeping or walking about distracted and hung over." One morning, after an all-night wedding, Antony arrived at the Forum so sick from drink that a friend had to hold his toga out of the way when he vomited. He hosted mimes, musicians, and prostitutes at al fresco dinners and rode in a chariot pulled by lions.

When it was rumored that Caesar had been killed in Spain and his enemies were marching toward Rome, Antony, again dressed as a servant, went incognito to see Fulvia, telling his wife that he had a note from her husband. When she asked whether Antony was dead, he threw off his disguise, put his arms around her and kissed her. Plutarch's tone is neutral as he describes this "boyish jest," the practical joke that Antony played in the hope of making Fulvia "more lighthearted." The modern reader may be struck by the aggression, if not the outright cruelty, of a man tricking his presumably loving wife into believing that he was dead: a joke unlikely to make a woman more lighthearted.

Though Plutarch refuses to blame Antony for the start of the war with Pompey, he holds him at least partly responsible for the murder of Caesar. During a drunken celebration, Antony insisted on crowning Caesar with a diadem woven with laurel, and though Caesar deflected the gesture, it convinced his enemies that he intended to declare himself king. After Caesar's assassination Antony went into hiding, reappearing in disguise as a servant. Soon after, he would give the dramatic funeral oration that moved the Romans to burn Caesar's body and attack the Forum.

Following the death of Julius Caesar, Antony, Octavian, and the Roman general Marcus Aemilius Lepidus went to war against Caesar's assassins. Both sides sought Cleopatra's allegiance, and after some delay—suggesting that her decision was more of a political than an emotional one, more about cautiously securing the future of Egypt than avenging her married lover—she dispatched her fleet to Greece in support of those who had been loyal to Caesar. She herself outfitted her navy and served as its commander, an assumption of power that would have startled the Romans, with their narrow view of a woman's role. It might even have surprised her fellow Egyptians, who were unused to seeing a queen prepared to lead her ships into battle. A combination of bad weather and Cleopatra's seasickness conspired to keep the Egyptian navy from participating in the fighting.

By then, Brutus and Cassius, two of the assassins, had been defeated at the Battle of Philippi. Three hundred men believed to be political enemies were killed, and the victors, having formed the so-called Second Triumvirate, assumed control of the Senate and the empire.

Reading Plutarch, one can watch him weighing the balance of strength and weakness, vice and virtue, good and bad fortune in the men about whom he writes. Ultimately, in his *Life of Antony*, he comes up against the event that for him tips the scales toward a harsher and more negative view of his subject.

That turning point occurs during the formation of the Second Triumvirate. Each of the three men was required to sacrifice an ally to be murdered by one of the others. Octavian turned Cicero over to Antony, Antony gave up his uncle Lucius Caesar, and Lepidus either murdered his brother Paulus or had him killed. "Nothing, in my opinion," writes Plutarch, "has ever surpassed the cruelty and savagery of this barter; for in this trading of murder for murder they were equally guilty of the lives they surrendered and of those they seized, though they were even guiltier in the case of their friends, whom they murdered without even hating them."

Antony seems to have taken special satisfaction in silencing Cicero. He ordered that the orator be decapitated, and his right hand — which had written so much and so vituperatively against Antony — be cut off. Antony is said to have burst out laughing when the severed head and hand were brought to him. It will be remembered that when Ptolemy XIII's men brought Caesar the head of Pompey, his former friend, ally, and relative, and only later his enemy in a civil war, he turned away and wept. But Mark Antony had no love for the man who had had his stepfather put to death and later led the Senate to declare him an enemy of the state, and he ordered these ghoulish trophies displayed in the Forum.

Plutarch is now on his way to building his case against Antony, who, in his position as triumvir, seized and installed himself in Pompey's former home. Refusing to meet government officials and ambassadors, he hosted "mimes, jugglers, and drunken flatterers" and carried on in a way that his fellow Romans saw as an insult to the spirit of Pompey, who had been a serious military and disciplined political leader. Later, Plutarch will use the excessive luxury and expense of Cleopatra's hospitality as yet another mark against her. But it is clear that these aspects of Antony's character were apparent well before his affair with Cleopatra. The lovers would encourage and (as we would say now) enable each other's tendency toward dissipation and extravagance, behaviors unlikely to endear them to their subjects.

For this, at least, we have evidence, one of Plutarch's primary sources: Philotas of Amphissa, a friend of Plutarch's grandfather, who had studied medicine in Alexandria. Friendly with a cook in Cleopatra's kitchen, he was the source of a story about the debauched excesses of Cleopatra's hospitality. Before a dinner that Cleopatra was hosting with Mark Antony, Philotas's friend noticed eight wild boars turning on spits and assumed the party would be huge. No, said the cook. There were only twelve guests. But the meal had to be flawless, regardless of when it was served, so multiple dinners had to be made — multiple boars roasted — to ensure that everything would be cooked to perfection whenever Antony and Cleopatra decided they were hungry. One wonders if this story was known outside the palace, and if so what effect it had on the suffering Egyptians still paying off the expenses of war, the debt to Rome, the taxes.

Later Philotas became one of the doctors treating Antony's son and after the collapse of the Ptolemaic dynasty, he moved to Delphi. A second anecdote he told Plutarch's grandfather concerned Antony's son, who gave Philotas some golden cups just for having made an amusing remark at dinner. Presumably, the story was included in the *Life of Antony* to illustrate how Antony's profligacy and the arrogance of his generosity were being passed down from father to son.

Through his *Life of Antony,* Plutarch offers us an ongoing and cumulative catalogue of his subject's flaws: Antony was wasteful in his spending; he robbed good people and diverted the money to flatterers and criminals; he seized an innocent person's house and gave it to his cook as a reward for a single delicious dinner. He was excessively trustful, almost simple, overconfident — but sincerely repentant when he knew he had done wrong. And yet, for Plutarch, all these faults pale beside "the crowning evil that befell him," the love for Cleopatra that awakened and fueled his own most excessive and wanton impulses, and corrupted him and overcame his better nature.

And so the hero surrenders to the witch and, unlike the more fortunate or cannier Odysseus, dies, still under her spell.

———

When the Second Triumvirate took control of the empire, the overseeing of Egypt was assigned to Antony, and through his envoy, Quintus Dellius, he summoned Cleopatra to a meeting at Tarsus.

They had met when she was "still a girl and ignorant of the world; but she was to meet Antony at the time of life when women's beauty is most splendid, and their intellects have fully matured. Hence she furnished herself with many gifts, much money, and such adornments as a woman of so wealthy a kingdom might afford, but she went placing her surest hopes in herself, and in her own magic arts and charms."

What did Plutarch mean by *magic arts and charms?* Did the words have the metaphorical meaning that they do today? The superstitious Romans, so heavily invested in auguries, oracles, and omens, would have been more likely to believe that she had employed witchcraft to make herself irresistible.

Cleopatra ignored Antony's summons, choosing instead "as if in mockery" to orchestrate her own arrival in a golden barge with purple sails, its oars beating in time to the music of flutes, fifes, and harps. By then it was known that a certain amount of pageantry had greeted and followed Antony throughout the most recent stages of his career. His Dionysian reception by the citizens of Ephesus—the women dressed as bacchantes, the men as satyrs— would have set a perverse sort of standard that Cleopatra might have felt obliged to equal or outdo.

En route to Tarsus, she lay under a canopy of gold cloth, dressed as the goddess of love, surrounded by boys, costumed as painted cupids, fanning her, and her maids, dressed like "Nereids and Graces, some stationed at the rudder, some at the ropes." The image conjured up is less of a ship than a parade float, an elaborate display in a Mardi Gras, Carnevale, or Tournament of Roses, but decorated with real gold and jewels, and with the queen of Egypt reclining at its center.

Lawrence Alma-Tadema's 1885 painting *The Meeting of Antony and Cleopatra, 41 BC,* is one of the few orientalist paintings in which Cleopatra appears fully clothed. In fact the queen is dressed somewhat modestly (possibly in deference to Victorian moral standards), in a pale blue gown with a leopard-skin cloak, lounging seductively under the canopy of her golden barge. Antony peers through the opening in the curtains at the woman who—the suggestion is implicit but unmistakable—will soon become his lover.

Plutarch describes the clouds of musky perfume that wafted from the ship to the shore as crowds lined the banks to watch the flotilla pass. He appears to be describing a combination of seduction, theatrical performance, military campaign, and religious rite: "And a rumor spread everywhere that Aphrodite had come to revel with Dionysus for the good of Asia." As we have already seen, the figure of Dionysus had a complex significance in the ancient world, in which the god was viewed both as a celebrant, a champion of debauchery and pleasure, and a dangerous and destructive force, a melding of Egyptian and Greek gods. One can't help wondering whether this "rumor" would have reached Cleopatra's ears; surely she would have recalled that one of the names her father chose for himself was "the new Dionysus," and that his Dionysiac tendencies did nothing to endear him to the Egyptian people or inspire their confidence in his leadership.

Even Antony, apparently not the most perceptive of men, would have recognized that hers was no purely official or strictly diplomatic mission. Private dinners followed the queen's arrival, hospitality competitions between the pair so conclusively won by Cleopatra that Antony could only laugh at his own "rustic awkwardness."

What follows is an anecdote that must be pure invention, unless we suppose that their conversation was somehow overheard. Here it is in Dryden's translation of Plutarch: "She perceiving that his raillery was broad and gross, and savored more of the soldier than the courtier, rejoined in the same taste, and fell into it at once, without any sort of reluctance or reserve."

What are we to make of this? Is Plutarch implying that Cleopatra was like Antony, that she had been waiting for him to unleash the coarseness within her? Do we assume that the queen of Egypt loved dirty jokes? Perhaps, if she had spent time with Caesar at his villa or among her own courtiers. (In Shakespeare's *Antony and Cleopatra,* she and her ladies-in-waiting are remarkably bawdy.) Or does Plutarch mean that the queen—aware that her country was at risk because the Triumvirate had essentially handed Egypt over to Antony—adapted herself to her audience of one? Like so many women, she became, at least in this one detail, what a man wanted her to be. Or was the anecdote simply Plutarch's way of telling us that the lovers had found their soulmates?

Tellingly, this is the point at which Plutarch informs us that it was not Cleopatra's less than extraordinary beauty so much as her presence, the charm of her conversation, the bewitching (again, perhaps, in a dual sense) nature of everything she did, the musical voice in which she spoke more than seven languages, including the demotic Egyptian that none of her predecessors had bothered to learn, that proved irresistible.

When Antony left Fulvia, charging her to continue on his behalf his struggle with Octavian, he allowed himself to be carried off to Alexandria, in Dryden's words, "there to keep holiday, like a boy, in play and diversion, squandering and fooling away in enjoyments that most costly, as Antiphon says, of all valuables, time." Within the space of a paragraph, Antony has become Cleopatra's plaything, playmate, and love slave. "She kept him always under her wing, freeing him neither day nor by night."

Once again, we are reminded of the status of most Roman women. With few exceptions (two or three of whom were at one time married to Antony), women were passive, fettered, and generally ignored except in their roles as wives, mistresses, and mothers. The multilingual, intelligent, and brave young queen was, to Plutarch, Cicero, and other classical authors, not only an oddity but a seditious example for other women.

Charm. Bewitch. Beguile. Yet again, magic is the undercurrent beneath the narrative that Plutarch has begun to tell, the story of two strong people engaged in a romance of love and death, a tale so dramatic and intense that it inspired Shakespeare to borrow it, more or less whole, and has contributed to our apparently undying interest in Cleopatra.

Antony and Cleopatra play dice, drink, and hunt. Dressed as servants—this is the fourth time that Plutarch shows us Antony disguised as a member of the lower classes—the couple lurk outside windows and mock the people inside. The besotted general reacts good-humoredly to a joke that Cleopatra plays on him: after he boasts of his skill at fishing, she orders a servant to attach a salted fish from the far-off Black Sea to his line. When he reels in the obvious hoax, to the great amusement of those present, Cleopatra turns her prank into an occasion for flattery (for which Plutarch suggests she had a kind of genius) by telling Antony that his skill with a fishing rod is unimportant because he is meant to hunt cities and continents.

"While Antony was amusing himself with such child's play," he was informed that Fulvia had lost the battle with Octavian and that the Parthians were overrunning Asia. Awakening from the sweet dream he was sharing with Cleopatra, Antony headed for

Parthia, then changed course and sailed to Rome to help Fulvia. Plutarch—and Antony's circle, it seems—still could not forgive Fulvia for her ambition, her lack of womanly skills and feminine modesty.

Soon after Antony heard the rumor that Fulvia had started the war with Octavian in order to bring him home from Alexandria, she died, conveniently for Antony, who was now able to blame his wife for the conflict. Octavian seems to have found this convincing; in any case he seemed willing to agree that an overly ambitious and aggressive woman was responsible for their troubles.

Octavian and Antony agreed to divide the empire between them, an agreement cemented when Octavian proposed that Antony marry his beloved, widowed, virtuous, and *Roman* sister, Octavia.

The passage that follows this betrothal interrupts Plutarch's account of the exploits, virtues, and failings of his hero to offer us something reminiscent of Renaissance drama, or a nineteenth-century novel. We might skim past it as we follow Antony, rushing off to make peace with Sextus Pompeius, Pompey's son, who was still unhappy about his father's death and was leading a fleet of pirate ships to plunder the coast of Sicily. But it is our introduction to Octavia, whose marriage to Antony would become immensely important as the story of Antony and Cleopatra was reworked by Shakespeare and others.

The element of the love triangle enters into the drama, with all its emotions: jealousy, rivalry, grief. This turn in the story will be used to give the Egyptian queen the feelings of a woman as opposed to the thoughts of ruler, who might sensibly worry that Antony's marriage might weaken her political influence on him and, by extension, on Rome. Antony, now a widower, will not deny his passion for Cleopatra but will not marry her because his reason was "still battling with his love for the Egyptian." And so Antony's struggle with himself and his own desires becomes a parallel narrative to his increasingly hostile conflict with Octavian.

After receiving a dispensation from the Senate that allowed Octavia to marry soon after her husband's death, she and Antony were wed. Plutarch may be unwillingly fascinated by Cleopatra, but he can praise Octavia, the ideal Roman woman, without reservation.

"Everyone was promoting this marriage, hoping that Octavia, who in addition to her great beauty had dignity and intelligence, would, when Antony came to know her, and she had won his heart (as such a woman naturally must), restore harmony between all parties and be their salvation." Indeed the marriage was extremely popular. It seemed — falsely, as it would turn out — an ingenious way of ensuring a lasting peace between two men whose enmity had threatened to weaken and divide the empire.

A problem that dramatists and filmmakers have grappled with ever since is how hard it is to avoid making Octavia more sympathetic than Cleopatra. With his preference for the virtuous and beautiful Octavia, Plutarch makes us see Cleopatra as the temptress whose hold on Antony, her ability to make him choose her over the superior Roman wife, can only be the result of recklessness, bad behavior, and the power of sex.

Complicating matters even further was the fact that around the time of Antony's marriage to Octavia, Cleopatra gave birth to twins. She named them Alexander Helios (the sun) and Cleopatra Selene (the moon), an immensely bold gesture that seems designed to increase the notoriety — and the outrage — that the children's birth occasioned.

At a banquet celebrating a diplomatic accord that Antony negotiated with Sextus Pompeius, the guests were said to have told jokes about Antony—newly married to one woman and in love with another, involved in a love triangle that his friends apparently considered comical.

In case we need more evidence that Cleopatra was cannier than her Roman lover, Plutarch tells us about the Egyptian soothsayer whom she sent along with Antony when he went off to battle the Parthians. Was it her idea? Did she convince Antony that he needed the services of a clairvoyant? The idea of the fortuneteller/soothsayer fit neatly into the ancient world's fervid interest in Egyptian magic, a fascination evident as far back as the book of Exodus, with its account of the pharaoh's court magicians turning rods into serpents.

The fortuneteller, who seems to have been all that Cleopatra could have wished, informed Antony that Octavian was not to be trusted. Neither Plutarch nor Antony seems to have suspected that Cleopatra might be the spirit voice speaking through the soothsayer, urging her lover to distance himself from the man who had brokered a marriage between Antony and Octavia. What better spy to have in the army of your distant, newly married lover than an Egyptian seer with the power to foretell the future and give Antony exactly the sort of advice that Cleopatra would have wanted him to have?

According to Plutarch, the soothsayer was good at his job, especially when his gloomy prognostications were confirmed by other dire portents. Antony consistently lost at cockfights and at the games of dice he played with Octavian's men. The rift between Antony and Octavian was widening, and Plutarch suggests, somewhat improbably, that Antony's annoyance and frustration over losing these games were what eventually turned his thoughts back to Cleopatra.

Meanwhile he left Italy and took Octavia and their baby daughter to spend the winter in Greece. In Athens, where he soon had a second daughter with Octavia, he lived in apparent contentment. Again, he referred to himself as Dionysus, drank heavily, consorted with musicians, and hosted lavish entertainments.

CHAPTER FIVE

The Final Act Begins

The tensions between Antony and Octavian intensified until Octavia attempted and succeeded in brokering a temporary rapprochement. With an eloquence that Plutarch intends to express her dignity and intelligence, she warned Octavian that were the conflict between him and her husband to continue, she would go from being the most blessed of women to the most wretched, and that regardless of which side triumphed, she would be the loser. Her pleas moved her brother's heart—indeed, the hearts of both combatants. In the spring of 37, the two men met in southern Italy; after an exchange of ships and soldiers, Antony left for Asia.

And so begins the last act in the story of Antony and Cleopatra. Like the fatal flaw that inevitably ruins the hero, like the snake in the garden waiting to sink its fangs into the hand that gathers the flowers, what Plutarch terms the "terrible mischief" that had lain dormant in Antony—the sinful fixation on Cleopatra from which he seemed to have been briefly distracted by his marriage to Octavia—was once again awoken. Plutarch goes on to blame the catastrophic failure of the Parthian campaign on Cleopatra, and Antony's ungovernable passion for her.

Antony again left for Syria to rejoin the struggle against the Parthians, and promptly sent for the Egyptian queen to join him in Antioch. Plutarch attributes his decision to the erotic hold that Cleopatra continued to maintain over him despite the years he had spent living in apparent domestic happiness with Octavia. But it seems equally likely that Antony understood that the Parthian army was large, skillful, and well equipped, and the backing and support of Egypt would be immensely useful—indeed crucial—in winning a victory against the Syrian aggressors.

Upon Cleopatra's arrival, Antony rewarded her with extravagant gifts of territory: Phoenicia, parts of Judea, Syria, much of Cilicia, a large part of the Eastern Mediterranean coast, and also Cyprus. The island where Cleopatra's uncle had killed himself rather than surrender his home to the Romans was now being returned. Indeed, much of the land that had belonged to the early Ptolemies—and been substantially reduced over the years—was now being restored to the Egyptian kingdom. Antony's gifts were not only romantic but strategic; the regions he bestowed on Cleopatra were rich in the natural resources that would allow him to expand his military capacities. Cleopatra responded by renaming herself "Queen Cleopatra, the Goddess, the Younger, Father-Loving and Fatherland-Loving"—a title intended to emphasize her new powers and prominence, as well as her continued loyalty to Egypt.

The Romans were furious at this willful disposition of their hard-won lands, and their outrage grew as Antony formally acknowledged the twins he had with Cleopatra, children who were now three and a half years old.

After sending Cleopatra back to Egypt, a journey that was for her a triumphal procession, Antony marched through Arabia and

Armenia, joined en route by an army — Romans, Iberians, Celts, Armenians — of more than a hundred thousand.

That fall, Cleopatra gave birth to her third son, whom she named Ptolemy Philadelphus.

In Plutarch's view, Antony's weakness for Cleopatra had already begun to undermine his better judgment. Running throughout his *Life of Antony* is the theme of excess, which seems to have been part of Antony's nature, a predilection unleashed early on by the influence of his friends. He and Cleopatra would bring it out in each other, like a form of flirtation or a sexual game involving escalating risks and dares. Beginning with their meeting on Cleopatra's golden barge, they made a point of outdoing each other in everything from the generosity of their gifts to the lavishness of their hospitality to the confidence they had in their increasingly rash decisions.

The recurrence of this love, like a malarial fever, so sickened Antony that as the Parthian expedition continued and faltered, its leader (according to Plutarch) could no longer think clearly and seemed unable to concentrate on waging war. One reason why the specter of Cleopatra hovers so ominously over Plutarch's narrative of the Parthian campaign may be that Plutarch is thought to have used as his source an eyewitness account of the expedition written by Antony's friend, the slippery and ambitious Quintus Dellius, whose relationship with Cleopatra was believed to have been one of a barely tempered mutual hostility. His involvement with the couple had begun early on when he was sent to persuade the queen to meet Antony at Tarsus.

There is an undying appetite for cautionary tales about men who destroy themselves for a woman. And so, Plutarch tells us, everything Antony did was done thoughtlessly, like a man with no control, who, "under the influence of certain drugs or enchantments . . . was forever glancing in her direction and thinking more of his speedy return than of conquering his enemies." We have returned to the realm of magic, to the catastrophic effects of a spell so powerful that all Antony's experience as a general and a military strategist deserted him.

What follows in Plutarch's *Life of Antony* is an annotated list of the bad decisions a commander makes when his mind is not focused on the war. Almost by accident, Antony won several victories, but the costs were disastrous. A brave and talented officer, Flavius Gallus, emerges out of the narrative only to be pierced with four arrows in a battle that killed three thousand men and wounded five thousand more.

Antony's sympathy and care for his wounded soldiers was so heartfelt and moving that Plutarch was again won over, swayed by the devotion of Antony's men. Their loyalty had many reasons, such as "his noble birth, his eloquence, the simplicity of his manners, his munificent generosity, and his lively and gracious conversation; and at the present time, by sharing the toils and sorrows of those suffering, and giving them whatever they needed, he made the sick and wounded more eager for duty than the healthy."

Though Plutarch was highly critical of Antony, increasingly so as Antony allowed his vices to overpower his virtues and permitted his strengths to be subverted and dismantled by Cleopatra's influence, passages such as this reveal something beyond simple respect and admiration for Antony's capability as a military leader. They suggest a response closer to genuine admiration for the hero's generous, expansive, fatally flawed character. The modern reader might add to this accounting of Antony's strengths the fact that at a time when Roman women were considered incapable of owning property or of making their own decisions, Antony married or was involved with Fulvia, Cleopatra, and Octavia, three of the era's (or any era's) most powerful and self-activated women.

Of course that was not what endeared him to Plutarch. His fondness was for the man's man, the leader beloved by his men. That particular vein of affection would run through the portraits of Antony that followed, in Shakespeare and up until our own time.

Here, for example, in *Octavian, Antony and Cleopatra* (1934) the British historians W. W. Tarn and M. P. Charlesworth offer a complex, nuanced, rounded, and ultimately forgiving portrait:

> Though [Antony] remained a blunt and jovial soldier, the darling of his troops, whom he understood and cared for, he had some statesmanlike qualities; in politics at Rome since Caesar's murder he had shown rapidity of decision and resource. . . . But his nature was full of contradictions. Cruel enough when roused, he was soon returned to his usual good nature; sometimes great in adversity, in prosperity he preferred luxury and amusement; straightforward and often loyal himself, he trusted others and was easily flattered and deceived. His worst trouble was women; they existed, he believed, for his pleasure, and they gave him ample reason for his belief. . . . Though he desired power, it was largely for the sake of pleasure; hence he himself might have been content with half the world, had he not been caught between two stronger forces.

No remotely similar passage appears in the classical histories about Cleopatra. Though more recent biographers — Roller, Grant, and Schiff, among others — have catalogued her extraordinary achievements and made strong cases for her ambition, intelligence, capability, and courage, for the confidence and resourcefulness with which she fought to preserve her dynasty during the final two decades of its existence, no one (with the possible exception of Shakespeare) has made a case for her having displayed the sort of human warmth for which Antony has been credited. No longer vilified, as she was for so many centuries, she is now respected — but respect is not the same as sympathy. Much has been made of her charm, but again, charm is not to be confused with humanity, and besides, her charm is mostly seen as having been weaponized against the powerful and hapless men who wandered into her sights. Plutarch's grudging fascination with her, especially near the end of his *Life of Antony,* fails to find in her anything nearly as moving as the empathy and love that Antony showed for his soldiers.

Literature offers many portraits of her as a libertine and a seductress, but nowhere among the classical authors do we find a scene of her interacting with the children she clearly cared so much about and went to such lengths to protect. All we know about her relationship with Caesarion concerns her attempts to have him acknowledged as Caesar's son and designated as her successor. Not until the 1963 film *Cleopatra* does Caesarion (who in the film appears to have been an only child) assume a major role — a part that turns on several historical inaccuracies. In the film, Julius Caesar is seen cooing affectionately over the infant that in life he never acknowledged as his own. And by the time of Cleopatra's death, her on-screen son is a handsome, curly-haired boy of about thirteen, when in fact he was eighteen when his mother died, still, at the very last, attempting to make him her heir.

As the Parthian campaigns deteriorated further, each catastrophe outdid the last for sheer carnage and horror. Antony's soldiers suffered a famine so severe they were forced to dig for roots and forage wild food, among them an herb that killed them after driving them mad. Once they had eaten the herb, the soldiers entirely lost their memory and busied themselves in moving heavy rocks from place to place, as if it were the most important task in the world. Ambushed by the Parthians, maddened by thirst, the survivors drank from a polluted river and became desperately ill. In the battle that followed, Antony lost thousands of soldiers, both from disease and injuries.

Antony's failure of leadership was so drastic that it would have been obvious to him that his military career was essentially over. And perhaps he could have retired to Alexandria with Cleopatra if he had not been drawn into another war — a death match against Octavian, a conflict that would not only doom the lovers but would put an end to Egypt's independence.

Thousands more soldiers perished as Antony marched through the wintry landscape of Armenia, arriving at last on the shores of the Mediterranean, where he awaited Cleopatra. Once more, Plutarch includes the sort of telling detail that suggests he either invented the incident he needed or was in possession of a firsthand account. Though Antony attempted to temper his impatience and anxiety by indulging in yet more drunken revelry and carousing, he kept leaping up from the table to see if Cleopatra had arrived.

Finally, her ship sailed into port, where she distributed money and clothing to her lover's battered and demoralized soldiers, and where Antony attempted to frame his disastrous defeat in the Parthian campaign as a victory.

A summons from the king of the Medes promised Antony that he would contribute heavily to a renewed campaign against the Parthians. But before Antony could leave, Octavia reentered the story, this time as a pawn in Octavian's scheme to intensify his conflict with Antony.

When the loving wife and mother asked her brother for permission to rejoin her husband, Octavian agreed — not, according to Plutarch, because he wanted to make his sister happy but rather because he suspected that Antony would mistreat her and was seeking an additional grievance against his fellow triumvir. Again, Octavia is hugely sympathetic, a loyal, patient, selfless, long-suffering Roman wife who—we know from the start—could not possibly hope to triumph against the wicked Egyptian seductress.

Stopping in Athens en route to rejoin her husband, Octavia received a letter from Antony telling her to stay where she was because he was heading inland with his army. And now Plutarch's narrative moves briefly into Octavia's point of view, and we can watch this intelligent, thoughtful woman hoping against hope, knowing one thing and doing another. Realizing that Antony was not entirely honest—spies would have told her that Cleopatra was with him—this wronged and decent woman asked where she was supposed to send a huge amount of baggage: gifts, clothes, pack animals, and two thousand soldiers she was planning to bring for her husband's army.

Plutarch's point of view shifts to focus on Cleopatra, who for the first time seems to have grown insecure. Worries have begun to plague her over the years since she gained Julius Caesar's help against her brother and sailed in her golden barge to persuade Antony to reconsider the imperious summons to Tarsus. (As Shakespeare reminds us, she was no longer young. In fact she was almost twenty years older than when she had charmed Caesar.)

And so Plutarch gives us the passage with which this book begins. Preparing for war with her lover's wife, fearing Octavia's nobility and devotion, Cleopatra "pretended" to be madly in love with Antony. She ramped up the romantic drama, acting as if she were trying not to let him see that she had been weeping. She instructed her servants to ask him how he could be so hard-hearted, how he could favor a woman who had married him only to please her brother over one who adored and depended on him, and who would die without him. She even went on a diet for him—the ultimate act of devotion.

Antony was helpless against her wiles. The fear that she might kill herself is suggested to have been among the possible reasons for his return to Alexandria. From this distance, we cannot speculate on Antony's motives, but we can imagine Antony being attracted not merely by desire for the newly thin Cleopatra and the exciting drama that surrounded her but by the prospect of having as an ally a woman who—unlike his loving, devoted wife—had vast wealth and a steady supply of natural resources at her disposal, and who was, in addition, a skilled and experienced military and naval tactician.

He was by that point a general who had not only lost critical battles but suffered humiliating defeats. The continuation of his conflict with Octavian may have seemed inevitable, and he would have welcomed the prospect of the Egyptian queen's aid and advice. On the other hand, his resistance to the likelihood (or the possibility) that a stable marriage to Octavia might have helped to bring about a lasting peace supports the argument that Plutarch has been making from the start: that Antony was under Cleopatra's spell, bewitched by her occult powers of seduction.

As Octavian predicted, his sister was spurned by her faithless husband and returned to Rome, where she nonetheless pleaded with Octavian not to resume his war against Antony. She said she would understand if her brother had his own reasons for fighting his former ally, but the conflict should not be about Antony's choosing Cleopatra over her. It would, she said, be ignoble to hear that the world's greatest leaders went to war over a woman, one motivated by passion for Cleopatra, the other by resentment.

Despite her brother's orders that she leave her errant husband's house, she refused to abandon the home that she had shared with Antony. Unlike her Egyptian rival, with her threats and theatrics, Octavia behaved with impeccable dignity, living in Antony's former residence and raising their children. She calmly played host to Antony's supporters, serving as an intermediary between the emissaries who came to Rome and her powerful brother. And in the process she inadvertently turned the Romans against a weakling and a libertine who could desert his model wife for the sinful Egyptian queen.

Plutarch is characteristically attuned to the ways in which private behavior influences public opinion, and the extent to which Antony's desertion of Octavia fueled the Romans' suspicions about his plans for the future of the empire. Yet Plutarch leaves us no room to question Octavia's motives when he reassures us that this decent woman never intended her grace and forbearance to add to Antony's shame.

Thus the triumvir's sister and the general's wife succeeding in taking a higher, more measured, and more admirable view of the situation than either her brother or her husband. Regardless of the outcome, we could say that at this point in the *Life of Antony* — and in the history of Cleopatra — the two principal women are not only smarter but wiser than the two leading men, who cannot think beyond the traditional, reflexive grab for land and power, the zero-sum imperative of kill or be killed.

Meanwhile, Octavia's phrase — "unless [Octavian] has his own reasons" — was a significant one. Plutarch suggests that Antony's mistreatment of his wife was merely a pretext for Octavian's continued aggression. Outrage on his sister's behalf may have fueled Octavian's suspicion and resentment; again, we cannot know. But whether or not we believe that the women maintained some responsibility and control, or merely were pawns in a game that would have been played without them, we can be certain that the two rivals for Antony's affection had a much higher degree of agency than that experienced by most women of their time.

From this point on, we can watch the brilliant Egyptian queen make a series of decisions that appear, especially in contrast to her earlier and cannier exercises of statecraft, to have been motivated by forces that seem more irrational, more emotional, and ultimately more desperate than anything she had done so far. She appears to have gone along with Antony's attempts to shore up his pride, to portray himself as a victor, to prove himself capable of defeating Octavian, and to deny the failure of his recent military ventures — efforts at saving face that Cleopatra surely would have known had only a distant and tangential relation to the reality of his situation.

In the autumn of 34, Antony and Cleopatra further enraged Octavian and the Roman public by staging an immensely elaborate and spectacular ceremony that would come to be known as the Donations of Alexandria. The occasion, it was claimed, was intended as a celebration of Antony's victory against the king of Armenia.

Seated on a golden throne, Cleopatra was invited to view a procession featuring the spoils and captives taken during the war, among them the Armenian king, who put something of a damper on the festivities by refusing to kneel before the Egyptian queen. Nonetheless, Antony joined his lover on a golden throne of his own and proclaimed her the "Queen of Kings" and "the New Isis," emphasizing her association with the Egyptian goddess, a connection that Cleopatra had maintained since the early years of her reign. Cleopatra was costumed as the goddess, while Antony is said to have dressed as Dionysus, whose significance in the Hellenistic cosmology and the career of Antony we have already seen.

Cleopatra's four children also occupied golden thrones, and

Caesarion was designated the "King of Kings," a title that Antony also gave to his own two sons with Cleopatra. The children were elaborately, even absurdly, costumed as they came forward to receive the gifts of territory that were being bestowed on them. Alexander Helios was given Armenia, Media, and — assuming that his father would be more victorious there in the future than he had been in the past — Parthia. Dressed as a mini–Alexander the Great, Ptolemy Philadelphus received Syria, Phoenicia, and Cilicia, while his twin sister, Selene, was awarded a portion of Cyrene (now Libya).

The ceremony was a peculiar one, one of the succession of ill-considered actions that the couple would take in these, their last years. Not only did the lands they distributed not belong to them, but the wisdom of giving the countries to children was questionable. Was Cleopatra tired of placating Rome? Did she and Antony imagine that it was time to provoke a war that they could win? Had they already begun to feel that they were being cornered and saw the Donations as a public proclamation and a private vow of their commitment to each other? The Donations of Alexandria marked a kind of watershed moment, after which the conflict with Octavian grew steadily more heated and the distance between Egypt and Rome began to appear unbridgeable.

Whatever its true purpose, the event could only have been interpreted as an insult and a provocation by Rome, and in that it was certainly successful. It spiked Octavian's antipathy toward Antony, and the Romans' distrust of Cleopatra's territorial and political ambitions. It suggested that Antony's deepest loyalty was not to Rome but to Egypt. One could say that it paved the way for the debacle — the downfall — that would eventually ruin the all-too-human couple who went to such lengths to establish their godlike status.

The popular disapproval of Antony's conduct as a husband was exacerbated by the contempt that Antony accrued when Octavian brought the Senate news of the Donations of Alexandria: the ridiculous pomp, the pointless exhibitionism, and the implicit (or explicit) affront to Rome.

In the aftermath of the Donations, Antony and Octavian traded escalating insults and accusations. Octavian insisted that Antony and Cleopatra had been illegally wed while Antony was still married to Octavia. Predictably, and for obvious reasons, he dismissed Cleopatra's claim that Caesarion was Caesar's designated heir. Again, one wonders why it did not occur to Cleopatra that her fight to establish her half-Egyptian son as Julius Caesar's legitimate successor was not only destined to fail but would effectively seal her son's doom.

Roman polemicists stepped up their attacks on Cleopatra, citing the decadence and debauchery of her court and her alleged use of magic to seduce and control Antony. One of Octavian's allies, Gaius Calvisius Sabinus, was charged with having stolen twenty thousand scrolls from the library of Pergamon and presenting them to Antony and Cleopatra during a banquet at which Antony had further unmanned himself—if such a thing were possible—by standing and rubbing his mistress's feet.

Meanwhile, Cleopatra was obliged to carry out the day-to-day duties and attend to the responsibilities necessary for the functioning of her kingdom. The sole example of what is believed to have been her handwriting—her autograph on a papyrus exempting one of Antony's associates from a tax on the land he owned and on the wheat and wine he was importing—is believed to date from this otherwise unsettled and presumably anxious period.

When a new outbreak of hostilities with Octavian seemed inevitable, Antony traveled to Ephesus, where he and Cleopatra assembled and outfitted a substantial army and navy. According to Plutarch, Cleopatra furnished her lover with two hundred ships, enough provisions to feed his entire army, and a generous sum of money.

Though Antony tried to persuade Cleopatra to return home, she is said to have feared that Octavia's attractions might seem more vivid if she herself were absent. She persuaded Antony that it would be wiser to keep her with him as an adviser; after all, it was she, and not Octavia, who had the experience of waging a war and governing a kingdom. One can easily imagine that this would have appealed to Antony: the company of a loyal and powerful supporter who, he trusted, would help him plan what promised to be a difficult conflict, a struggle that would have seemed doubly challenging in the wake of his recent defeat in Parthia.

From Ephesus, Antony and Cleopatra sailed to the island of Samos and there distracted themselves with yet more merrymaking. Oxen were sacrificed. Companies of actors and musicians were imported from throughout the empire and assembled so that, notes Plutarch, "while nearly all the world around was filled with groans and lamentations, this one island for many days resounded with piping and harping, theaters filling, and choruses competing. . . . And men began to ask themselves how the conquerors would celebrate their victories, when they held such extravagant festivities at the opening of the war."

Distraction may have been their principal purpose, as Cleopatra and Antony endeavored to forget what the worsening conflict with Octavian might portend for their future. We can assume that the Egyptian queen was behind Antony's request for a formal divorce from Octavia, a provocation that would hardly have been in Antony's best interests. But though this has been seen as a demand for an outward show of loyalty from an increasingly possessive lover, again we cannot estimate how much of Cleopatra's strategy was based on a sensible desire to secure some margin of safety for herself, her children, and her country. By this point the official and public sentiment in Rome was running so strongly against Cleopatra that she might well have feared that any reconciliation between Antony and Octavia — and, by extension, Octavian — might have meant that her lover and his former enemy would now unite all Rome against her.

Next the couple visited Athens for another round of festivities. There Cleopatra tried, without much success, to turn the public opinion against Octavia, who was popular in the city. This was only one of the ill-conceived efforts and unwise decisions that the couple made during this period, actions that suggest that emotion rather than calculation guided their behavior. It was not in Antony's, or anyone's, best interest to insist, as he did now, that Octavia be evicted from their house in Rome. We can only assume the Egyptian queen was behind a move that could only have been motivated by a lover's jealousy rather than a sensible concern with public relations.

Taking all the children except Antony's son with Fulvia, who was in Athens with his father, Octavia left their house, weeping. She feared that she might be seen as one of the causes of the war, and again she garnered great sympathy from the Romans, though Plutarch notes that it was Antony whom the people pitied most, on account of his enslavement by the Egyptian queen.

Plutarch now ticks off the succession of mistakes that led to Antony's defeat. The first was the time that he squandered in merrymaking, an interval that gave Octavian, who had been unprepared for a full-scale war, ample opportunity to get ready. These preparations were accomplished partly through the levying of harsh and unpopular taxes earmarked for funding the army and navy.

Though he loved and was loved by his soldiers, Antony seems to have been unwise in his choice of close associates and confidants. Quintus Dellius would go over to Octavian's side in the hope of catching a more favorable wind, and he was not the only one; Antony's secretary, Lucius Munatius Plancus, returned to Rome with the suggestion that Octavian look into Antony's last will and testament. That document may well have been a forgery, so perfectly did it play into the fears of the Romans. The senators to whom Octavian read the will aloud were horrified by the clause directing that after Antony's death his body should be sent to Alexandria, even if he died in Rome. Echoing the rumors that had once concerned the relationship between Julius Caesar and Cleopatra, it was now said that Antony was conspiring to move the capital of the empire from Rome to Alexandria.

Still more disparaging gossip spread throughout Rome, offering evidence that his submission to Cleopatra had left Antony unfit to perform his political and military duties. Purportedly Antony had paused in the middle of a trial in the tribunal to read the love notes, inscribed on onyx and crystal, he had received from Cleopatra. It was claimed that he left another trial halfway through to follow and cling to the edge of the golden litter in which Cleopatra was being carried through the Forum.

A friend of Antony's, Geminius, traveled to Greece to ask Antony to take action before he was declared an enemy of the Roman people, but Cleopatra allegedly suspected him of working for Octavia. At one drunken dinner, he was required to confess what had really brought him to Greece, and when he claimed to be too drunk to answer except to suggest that everything would improve if Cleopatra were sent back to Egypt, Antony flew into a rage and Cleopatra remarked that Geminius was lucky to have escaped being tortured.

Given the fresh volley of insults that Octavian directed at Antony—that he should officially give up the power he had already surrendered to a woman, that he was under the influence of drugs, presumably administered by Cleopatra—it is little wonder that sweat flowed unceasingly and portentously from a marble sculpture of Antony at Alba. Other evil omens followed. A city that Antony had colonized disappeared into a sinkhole. In the Acropolis, statues of the gods most sacred to Antony and Cleopatra were struck by lightning. Most ominous of all, a flock of swallows built their nests on Cleopatra's flagship, only to be driven off by other swallows, who destroyed the baby birds.

The armies prepared to face off. Antony is said to have amassed five hundred ships, one hundred thousand soldiers, and twelve thousand horsemen. Allies were summoned from Libya, Cilicia, Cappadocia, Thrace, and elsewhere and enlisted to fight on Antony's side. Octavian was less well armed and prepared, with fewer ships but more soldiers than his opponent.

And now Antony prepared to make the mistake that would seal his doom—a critical misjudgment that Plutarch and history would blame on the bad advice and the insidious influence of Cleopatra. Although Antony had a numerical naval advantage, his ships were less efficiently constructed and less well equipped for battle—and his sailors less well trained—than Octavian's, and in Plutarch's view, it was Antony's position as a "mere appendage" of Cleopatra that made him go along with her insistence that the war be waged at sea.

And so we approach the Battle of Actium, a name that resonates throughout history, like that of other turning points, critical victories and defeats: Waterloo, Hastings, Little Big Horn, Gettysburg. The Battle of Actium marked a major turn—a downward one—in Cleopatra's fortunes.

After Actium, the narrative veers toward the tragic, and the story of Cleopatra's life becomes one of defeat, betrayal, more betrayal, anguish, and desperation, all the more powerful because we know nothing of what she thought, and almost nothing of what she said, and so we must intuit her growing panic and fear almost entirely from the evidence of what the Egyptian queen did.

In the lead-up to the fighting, Octavian made several attempts to defuse hostilities, overtures to which Antony responded with contempt and insults that included a suggestion that the two leaders settle matters by engaging in hand-to-hand combat. Antony's most trusted advisers counseled him to send Cleopatra away and, taking into account the superior strength of his infantry and his relative inexperience in naval warfare, to wage the war on land. But Cleopatra prevailed, not (according to Plutarch) out of concern for Antony but because she had already anticipated defeat and was eyeing her own most expeditious exit strategy.

Engineering a disastrous military defeat seems like a recklessly elaborate and foolish way for a clever queen to rid herself of a lover, even one who may have begun to become an encumbrance. Later she would try to persuade Octavian that she preferred him to Antony. We can imagine that as he prepared to meet Antony at Actium, Octavian would have seen the obvious advantages of Cleopatra's defection, which might in fact have ended the war. And Cleopatra would have known that. One of the puzzles that can never be solved is the question of why she encouraged Antony to wage a war in a way that she must have suspected would guarantee a loss.

Lacking enough sailors to man them, Antony set fire to over a hundred Egyptian ships and ignored the entreaties of a centurion who had fought in many of his wars and begged him to fight this one on land. Inclement weather forced a delay of several days, but at last the battle began. The heavily armored ships crashed into one another, the confrontation seeming less like a naval engagement than an assault on a walled city. Though Antony's ships were bulkier and more heavily fortified, Octavian's were swifter and capable of surrounding — and attacking — each of Antony's ships with several of their own.

And then the unthinkable happened — or in any case the unpredictable, to anyone, of course, but Cleopatra. Her sixty ships unfurled their sails, sliced through the front lines, and fled the battle, heading toward the Peloponnese. When Antony saw what was happening, he turned his own ship and followed Cleopatra.

> Here it was that Antony made clear that he was governed by the motives not of a leader or of a brave man, or even by his own judgment; instead, just as someone jokingly said that the soul of a lover lives in someone else's body, he was dragged along by the woman as if he had been born part of her, and must go wherever she went. For as soon as he saw her ship sailing away he forgot everything, betrayed and ran away from those who were fighting and dying for him, and went . . . to pursue the woman who had already begun his ruin and would in due course complete it.

Plutarch cannot get over it. Antony is beyond forgiveness, and Plutarch can only respond by shrinking the powerful Roman to the size of a homunculus: a captive soul. Antony has been deprived of all agency, wrecking his career and his reputation, and about to end his life as an Egyptian queen's humiliated love slave.

In the Roman era — perhaps in any time — little could be more shameful or shocking than a leader deserting his men and following a woman. In the first century BCE, Antony's act may have seemed more extreme than it might today; it was certainly more unusual, given the low status and the low regard for Roman women. But there has never been a time when the world has applauded a man who did what Antony did. Incidences of male leaders sacrificing everything for a woman have been rare enough to count on one hand. A furor greeted Edward VIII's abdication of the British throne in 1936 for love of the American divorcée Wallis Simpson. And he was simply stepping out of the line of succession, not leaving a fleet of armored ships and thousands of sailors to die. Antony's soldiers, many of whom had experienced his compassionate and responsible leadership, were at first unable to believe that he had deserted them, and remained at their posts for ten days, until, abandoned by their general, Publius Canidius Crassus, they went over to Octavian's side.

The story contributed to the myth of the freakishly powerful and destructive Cleopatra, the woman whom Dante consigned to hell and whom later writers would condemn for her greed, cruelty, and excess. Actium is the turn in the narrative at which, for these writers, Cleopatra reveals her "true" nature as a woman capable of destroying a man—not just a man, but a Roman, not just a lover but a general and a triumvir. She may well have ordered the deaths of two siblings and waged a war in which a third was killed, but this was different. If one is looking to make a case against the Egyptian queen—as many have—this is the event that reveals her potential for betrayal, and for evil.

Though Antony was taken aboard Cleopatra's ship, she failed to greet him, and they ignored each other. Instead—in yet another of Plutarch's details that suggests either the presence of an eyewitness or an active imagination—he went to the bow of the ship and sat alone, silently, holding his head in his hands. More than that of the prankster disguising himself as a servant, more even than that of the orator inciting his fellow Romans to violence after Caesar's murder, this image of Antony—alone, silent, holding his head, doubtless contemplating the end of his military career and quite possibly his life — is what stays with us.

Antony emerged from his isolation and misery only once, for a brief hostile confrontation with one Eurycles, a Spartan who threatened to hurl a spear at him from a nearby ship and announced that he was avenging the death of his father, whom Antony had beheaded as punishment for a robbery. Eurycles then attacked and seized another of Antony's admiral's ships, heavily laden with expensive household goods — an assault that could only have increased Antony's humiliation. Antony returned to his solitude and silence, refusing to speak to Cleopatra, though it was unclear whether he was angry at her or ashamed to be in her presence.

It was not until they docked at Taenarum, in the southern Peloponnese, that Cleopatra's maids brokered some sort of reconciliation between the lovers and they consented to eat and sleep together.

Meanwhile, at Actium, Antony's fleet acknowledged defeat.

The Battle of Actium furthered the expansion of the Roman Empire and effectively ended the increasingly shaky construct of an independent Ptolemaic Egypt. But despite centuries of speculation, no one has offered a conclusive explanation of why Cleopatra took her ships and sailed away.

Given her background and history, it would have been unlikely for her to flee out of sheer instinct and terror. Some have suggested that she had on board a significant amount of treasure that she was reluctant to sacrifice. It has also been theorized, not unreasonably, that when she saw that defeat was unavoidable, she decided to save her own life and whatever she could salvage. Why should she and her sailors die because of a factional quarrel between two Romans? Had it really been her idea to fight Octavian at sea? We will never know her reasons. We can surmise that her betrayal of Antony was unintentional, since his victory would have allowed her to survive and permitted her country's autonomy to endure at least for a while. Her future under Octavian's rule promised to be grim.

After his victory, Octavian traveled on to Athens, where he helped secure the loyalty of the Athenians by distributing what remained of the available grain supplies. Plutarch's great-grandfather Nicarchus, who was in Greece at the time, described the people's relief when they learned that Antony was no longer in charge since he had ordered his soldiers to whip the unfortunate laborers forced to carry grain to his ships.

Only when they reached the Libyan coast did Cleopatra finally head for Egypt. Antony remained alone, aimlessly wandering about, contemplating his recent losses and his uncertain future. By the time he returned to Alexandria, Antony—whose general in charge of his Libyan operations had gone over to Octavian—had decided to kill himself and was only dissuaded by the intercession of friends. Several times Antony would ask one of his men to kill him, a reckless and alarming request that would ultimately result in the grotesque nightmare of his death.

Cleopatra was forced to take control as Antony, succumbing to despair and defeat, retreated to a cottage he had built on the beach, where he planned to live out his life as a hermit. It is hard to imagine that this failed to warn Cleopatra that from then on Antony was likely to be more of a hindrance and a burden than a help.

Cleopatra's behavior suggests that she was becoming increasingly desperate. Until that point, she had acted with careful calculation, rather like an expert chess player plotting the succession of moves most likely to produce the most favorable outcome. But Antony's defection and dissolution appears to have shaken her confidence and resolve. Part of her brilliance as a politician had derived from her ability to identify and enlist the strongest and most dependable allies. But now it must have seemed as if there were no longer a visible or viable source of counsel, of either personal or military support — as if there were no one left to seduce or dazzle into coming to her aid.

However we may chafe at Shakespeare's portrayal of the thirty-nine-year-old queen as bordering on the geriatric, we can well imagine that having ruled for two decades, having survived the intense demands and pressures of her position, she may have felt tired. She had just fled a war in which her lover and principal ally had been ignominiously defeated, disgracing himself and destroying his reputation by running after a woman rather than remaining to fight alongside his men. And now he had retreated to a shack on the beach. For the first time since she had persuaded Julius Caesar to help her defeat her brother and allied herself with Antony, she was left to face the old threat — Roman imperial expansion — without an influential Roman to intercede on her behalf. And even as her independence, her survival, and the integrity of her country might have seemed threatened, she was still determined to ensure that her children would not be made to suffer or die along with her.

Her first instinct was to flee — to abandon the country she had loved, the people who had depended on her for two decades. She considered ordering her soldiers and sailors to drag her fleet across the isthmus that separated Egypt from the Arabian Sea. Even if it meant leaving Egypt forever, she might at least act as a sort of decoy, drawing Rome's fury to herself and allowing her children to continue to rule. Presumably she would take treasure with her, so Octavian would no longer be driven by greed for the gold and jewels he knew, or imagined, her to possess. But she could not seriously have believed that after everything that had occurred Rome would want to continue its relationship with its "friends and allies" among the Ptolemies.

Predictably, Cleopatra's escape plan proved impractical, and she had no choice but to throw in her lot with that of her despondent and progressively useless lover. On learning that his soldiers and supporters had deserted him and that he no longer had any power outside Egypt, Antony was persuaded to leave his hut and return to the royal palace. There he and Cleopatra distracted themselves with more banquets and feasts and together with their friends founded an ominous-sounding fellowship they called the "Partners in Death" — apparently a kind of mass suicide pact among associates who agreed that they were willing to die together.

Even as she prepared Caesarion to rule in her place and attempted to find a refuge to which she and Antony could flee, Cleopatra seems to have been preparing for death. She allegedly began to experiment with a variety of poisons, trying them out on condemned prisoners. Whether or not this story is true, it provided the subject for Alexandre Cabanel's monumental painting *Cleopatra Testing Poisons on Condemned Prisoners* (1887), a work that measures 65 by 110 inches, and a section of which adorns the cover of the 2010 Oxford University Press paperback edition of Duane W. Roller's biography, *Cleopatra*. Reclining diagonally across the image, Cleopatra could not be lovelier, a sensual dark-haired beauty, more or less naked to the waist, with pale, luminous breasts. Her crown is ornamented with a tiny cobra and around her plump hips are layers of filmy, brightly colored skirts. Her legs are stretched out in front of her, and she is reclining on one arm, languidly stretching the other along the top of her red and gold divan. On the carpet beside her is a leopard with glittering green eyes. Dangling a bouquet from her fingers, she gazes off to her right at something that in the cover detail we cannot see. We do see her naked arm, and a servant girl, also naked to the waist, fanning Cleopatra.

Invisible beyond this section of the painting, a man writhes on the ground in agony, and a dead man is being carted off by two attendants, his corpse sagging between them. *Cleopatra Testing Poisons on Condemned Prisoners* is an example of orientalism at its most egregious. The image is informing its viewers (or confirming them in their view) that life is cheap in the East, where, if a queen is thinking of killing herself, she can try out the poisons on human guinea pigs to find the least painful — or, if she's so inclined, the most tortuous — way to end a life. Cleopatra's beauty, her partial nudity, her sensuality, the brightness of the colors and her disregard for casual murder feeds into every stereotype that the West has ever created about the East, and offers further "evidence" to support the Roman sentiment that imperial conquest was a necessary solution to the excesses and evils endemic to Africa and Asia.

Even the idea of poison was considered suspect and Asiatic, though poisoning has been common throughout the West from antiquity to the current moment, most notably among the agents of Vladimir Putin. Despite the evidence to the contrary, poisoning has also been considered a particularly female means of committing suicide or eliminating an enemy, though in fact it appears to be an equal-opportunity weapon.

Cabanel's subject was not original. Plutarch goes on at length about Cleopatra's human and animal researches. Having formed and enrolled in her Partners in Death, she busied herself "collecting all sorts of deadly poisons and testing them for painlessness by having them administered to prisoners condemned to death. When she saw that the quick-acting ones induced painful deaths, while the gentler ones acted slowly, she next tried wild animals, observing them as they attacked one another. This she did every day; and by testing all of them she found that only the bite of the asp brought on a sleepiness and lethargy, without convulsions or groans, producing only a gentle sweat on the face, while the faculties were easily relaxed and clouded."

The painter could have chosen any of the scenes from Plutarch in which the queen appears. But this one excited his imagination — or perhaps he hoped its conflation of sex and death might be the most commercial. If we wonder why Cleopatra has been cast as an oversexed enchantress who traded her body for power and ruined the lives of two heroic men, we have only to look at this painting to understand why it was believed that she deserved the bite of the venomous snake. Conversely, it is hard to imagine this languorous, pretty girl rebuilding a city, winning a war against her brother, functioning as a diplomat, governing a country, and raising four children.

However we may discount the fantasies and projections of later painters and writers, evidence suggests that the subject of suicide — the quickest and least painful way to die — did hang heavily in the air of the royal place during Cleopatra's final months.

CHAPTER SIX

The Snake

Cleopatra and Antony grew increasingly desperate as they attempted to negotiate with Octavian, who after the couple's humiliating defeat at Actium had little reason to negotiate himself. Yet they continued to beg for mercy from a notoriously unmerciful opponent, whose record showed the lengths he would go to exact revenge. In the war against Caesar's assassins, a captive begged to have his body buried after he was executed, and Octavian said he would leave that matter to the birds. He ordered a father and son to decide which of them would die first, then killed them both, one after the other. Three hundred prisoners who pleaded for their lives were told, "You must die," and slaughtered. This militates against the idea, so important to Julius Caesar and others, that one measure of Roman superiority was the compassion that they—unlike their barbarian enemies—showed to their conquered foes.

Octavian's pressing concern in his dealings with Antony and Cleopatra was to ensure that the couple could not recoup their forces and continue the war. The odds against this might seem overwhelming unless we factor in the Romans' belief that the Egyptian queen was capable of magic. They also had some worry that the defeated couple might find a sanctuary in a region (possibly Gaul) that would accept them and, more to the point, welcome Cleopatra's gold. Octavian feared that her fortune might slip forever out of Rome's grasp.

As Antony grew more melancholy and less helpful, the queen seems to have understood that she was fighting not only for her country but for her life and the lives of her children. In Cassius Dio's account, Antony seems increasingly pathetic. Appealing to Octavian, man to man, he defended "his connexion with the Egyptian woman and recounted all the amorous adventures and youthful pranks that they had shared" (book 51), apparently forgetting that this was the last thing he should have been telling a leader who, despite his own infidelities, prided himself on being upright and moral.

All Antony's overtures to Octavian received responses that were, at best, sarcastic and dismissive. When Antony again offered to engage Octavian in hand-to-hand combat, Octavian replied that Antony would have to find another way of killing himself. Antony offered to commit suicide if Cleopatra were allowed to live. That he was said to have been suicidal since the defeat at Actium makes this voluntary self-sacrifice appear considerably less selfless and dramatic than it otherwise might.

Antony sent Antyllus, his son with Fulvia, to deliver a generous payment, which Octavian confiscated before sending Antyllus back with nothing to show for his efforts. Cleopatra's gifts to Octavian included a gold throne, a crown, and a scepter, signals of her willingness to cede her relative independence in return for . . . what? Underneath everything else was Rome's growing sense that Egypt was weak, its leadership chaotic, and could be had almost for the asking and with little loss of Roman life.

The annexation of Egypt would be a coup that would accomplish what Octavian's predecessors had only considered, a conquest that would be a step toward transforming himself from Octavian into the Emperor Augustus: the new title he would be given by the Senate in 27 BCE, three years after the death of Cleopatra.

Cleopatra appears to have tried every conceivable option. Perhaps she and Antony could live as private citizens and Egypt could be turned over to their children. In the unlikely hope that this might happen, Cleopatra stepped up her grooming of Caesarion as her replacement. The usually resourceful, savvy queen put wishful thinking above common sense, imagining that Octavian would welcome a king of Egypt whose mother had raised him to believe that he was Caesar's rightful heir.

Octavian and Cleopatra began to leave Antony out of their communications and to experiment with the notion of having Antony killed. It is unclear whether Octavian nurtured a special hatred for his former fellow triumvir, who had fallen in with the Egyptian woman and turned against him. Was Octavian simply toying with Cleopatra because he knew that he had already won? Did he imagine that she would believe that giving up Antony would mean that she would be spared — taken to Rome in chains as a human trophy, evidence of Octavian's triumph? Could he have imagined that this would be an option for her? Among the plot twists that have come to surround those terrible months is yet another unlikely detail: Octavian endeavored to convince Cleopatra that he had fallen in love with her, and that their romance would flourish if she joined him in Rome.

Even Plutarch, so disinclined to sympathize with Cleopatra, is moved by the escalating panic of those final months. He tells the story at length, pausing to introduce minor characters. Among them is Thyrsus, one of Octavian's freed men, who, though not terribly intelligent, was dispatched to Alexandria as a kind of spy, assigned to conspire with Cleopatra in a plan to eliminate Antony.

Cleopatra and Thyrsus spent so much time together, communicating in secret, that Antony grew suspicious, and had him whipped and returned to Octavian with a message that Thyrsus's insolence had irritated Antony at a time when he had plenty to be irritated about. There is something pitiful about the tone of this, as Antony blamed his beating of Thyrsus — a man whom he imagined was plotting with his lover to kill him — on his own moody instability. In addition, Antony told Octavian that he was now free to beat one of Antony's men to even the score.

Cleopatra responded to their worsening circumstances and her progressively more limited options by lavishing attention on Antony, who now must have seemed like a bargaining chip in her negotiations with Octavian. If the romance between Antony and Cleopatra was ever a love match, it was one no longer, though she celebrated his birthday with yet another lavish feast and generous gifts to the guests, who, according to Plutarch, sat down to dinner poor and went home rich.

Meanwhile Cleopatra began constructing a complex of elaborate tombs and mausoleums of gold and silver, ebony and ivory, encrusted with emeralds and pearls. She also amassed a supply of firewood and kindling, thus appearing to prepare for two different outcomes. She may have hoped that signaling her plans to incinerate her treasure might persuade Octavian to relent and reach some tenable agreement. Whatever the outcome, she would sooner or later need a tomb befitting her royal rank and glorious career. She owed it to herself and her country to die in a style befitting what she must have feared was the last Ptolemy.

As the war against Octavian sputtered on, Antony's victories were minor, temporary, and ultimately fruitless. When Antony beat back Octavian's advancing army, he returned to the palace, kissed Cleopatra, and presented his bravest soldier to her. Cleopatra rewarded the hero with golden armor, for which the soldier thanked her—and that same night he went over to Octavian's side.

According to Plutarch, Antony began telling his servants to ramp up the splendor of his feasts, increasing the pace and quantity of his already excessive drinking, for no one knew how much longer he could continue to live like this, or how soon they would be wining and dining a new master while he lay on the ground, a useless withered corpse. If these sentiments were indeed voiced by Antony or merely a general indicator of his mental state, did word of it get back to Cleopatra? The bleakness of his mood and his sentimental self-pity were unlikely to have made her feel that she could depend on his support.

One night, a loud and joyous noise that sounded like a procession of musicians and revelers was heard winding through the streets of Alexandria and out through the city gates. It was an ordinary occurrence, unless one were looking for omens, which the people of Alexandria were. The sudden appearance and precipitous exit of the merry band was interpreted to mean that the god Dionysus had deserted Antony, his devotee and in happier times his namesake.

From a hill overlooking the harbor, Antony watched his ships sail out to confront Octavian's, then immediately turn, switch sides, and join the opposing camp, so that both navies, combined now, were sailing into the port to attack him. When Antony's infantry soldiers realized what had occurred, they too deserted, allying themselves with Octavian.

Antony had prided himself on his close relations with his soldiers. He had commiserated with the wounded, grieved for the dead. Even Plutarch was moved by the respect and loyalty he received, and by the sympathy and profundity of the connection between a commander and his men. But now that loyalty had been severely tested. During the Parthian campaign, vast numbers of soldiers had died horrible deaths, partly as a consequence of Antony's misjudgment. The veterans and new recruits had seen with their own eyes, or had heard about, how he had abandoned his sailors and joined Cleopatra's retreat from Actium. Whatever their reasons, his legions were no longer willing to fight and die for him.

The rift between Cleopatra and Antony grew wider, uglier, and more public. After his army and navy deserted him, Antony was said to have rampaged through the city, blaming Cleopatra. Claiming to fear for her safety, she and her maids walled themselves up in her heavily fortified tomb. Now she was fighting on two fronts, against Octavian, her enemy, and against Antony, her lover. She instructed her servants to tell Antony that she was dead, and he was on his own: he could no longer depend on her, and there was no point in accusing her of having betrayed him.

Antony prepared to kill himself. He asked one of his servants, the aptly named Eros, to stab him with his own sword, but the loyal servant refused and killed himself instead. Antony reacted as if Eros had offered him a challenge by presenting him with a model of valor to be emulated. He promptly stabbed himself. But the wound did not prove fatal and stopped bleeding as soon as he lay down.

Ancient history is full of hideous deaths, poisonings, stabbings, assassinations. We have seen how the Ptolemies outdid the Greeks and Romans for the ingenuity, range, and remorselessness with which they ended family members' lives. But even among these tortured exits, Antony's death stands out for its gruesomeness and pathos: it was gory, painful, embarrassing, clownish, and hideously protracted.

Wounded, but not yet fatally, Antony begged to be put out of his anguish, but his servants and retainers fled, leaving him bleeding, until Cleopatra interceded and ordered him brought to her tomb. Either the door could not be opened or Cleopatra chose not to open it, so yet another indignity was added to those that Antony had already suffered. He was attached to a pulley made of ropes and cords and hoisted up to enter the tomb through a window.

The rescue did not go well. Witnesses described it as the most pitiful thing they had ever seen. Bleeding, struggling in his makeshift sling, Antony writhed and stretched out his arms to Cleopatra, who reached for him as she and her maids screamed and struggled to grab him and pull him inside the window. Below them a crowd had gathered, shouting encouragement and advice, weeping in horror and sympathy.

Overcome by the sight of her lover, who now appeared to by dying, Cleopatra laid him on the bed, beating her breast, smearing herself with his blood, calling him master, husband, commander, forgetting their differences and feeling only his imminent loss. Again we wonder who was there, who overheard and reported on the lamentations of the queen and the last words of a dying man. It has been suggested that Plutarch borrowed some of these details from the memoir of Cleopatra's doctor, but we will never know how much of this part of the story is fantasy or supposition, the work of Plutarch or someone else filling in the blanks in the horrific narrative.

Asking for wine, Antony told Cleopatra to watch out for herself and asked her not to pity him, because he had led a heroic life, had been happy, and was dying a noble death, as one Roman killed by another Roman. It may take a beat to realize that Octavian was not the murderous Roman he meant, but rather that Antony was referring to his suicide: he himself was the "other Roman." He advised Cleopatra to trust Proculeius, one of Octavian's friends.

Proculeius arrived at the tomb soon after Antony died. For even as Antony was being dangled and hoisted up to Cleopatra, one of his bodyguards had made off with the bloody sword that had wounded him and showed it to Octavian to prove that Antony was dying or dead.

Octavian responded much as his great-uncle had on hearing of the death of Pompey, with ceremonial weeping over the loss of his former ally, fellow triumvir, and relative by marriage – and in sharp contrast to Antony, who had burst out laughing over Cicero's butchered remains. But Octavian was not so overcome with grief that he did not think to quell in advance any ill will that might have been occasioned by the circumstances of Antony's death. He produced the communications he had exchanged with Antony and read them aloud to prove how conciliatory and friendly he had been, how coarse and hostile were Antony's answers. One marvels at his forethought in having kept and saved both sides of a correspondence.

Even in death, Antony had been grievously mistaken. Proculeius was not to be trusted, for he had been sent by Octavian to ensure that whatever happened, Cleopatra would not make good on her threat to destroy her treasure along with herself.

The ideal outcome from Octavian's point of view would be to entice Cleopatra to come to Rome, where she could be exhibited as a conquered enemy: the once great Cleopatra, the former queen of Egypt subdued by Octavian, exhibited among the spoils of war, possibly in chains, a testament to his power and the central showpiece of his glorious victory parade. Octavian's emissary was authorized to do what was necessary, using bribes, tricks, and promises, to separate Cleopatra from her gold and persuade her to travel to Rome. No one could have imagined that the queen would be foolish enough to fall for Octavian's rather crude deceptions, but the Roman general possessed an important, perhaps all-important, card to play in his deadly game with Cleopatra: her children, who were not entombed with her and were consequently at Octavian's mercy.

Speaking on the other side of the locked tomb door, Cleopatra asked that her children be protected. Proculeius advised her to trust in Octavian's mercy, a promise that turned out to be both true and false. Soon after Cleopatra's death, Caesarion and Antyllus would be killed; Cleopatra and Antony's children were spared and sent to Rome.

While another envoy took his place outside the door, negotiating with Cleopatra, the "trustworthy" Proculeius entered the chamber through a window and seized the queen. When her maids screamed a warning, she tried to stab herself with a dagger that was hidden in her clothes, but Proculeius encouraged her to entrust her life and safety to Octavian, his forgiving and merciful master. After making sure that she was not concealing any poisons, he left a guard behind to make sure that she stayed alive. The guards were instructed to keep her comfortable and calm while Octavian and his advisers decided what to do next.

While Cleopatra remained in her tomb, essentially buried alive, Octavian rode in triumph through Alexandria, reassuring the terrified citizenry that he was pardoning them, partly out of love for their beautiful city and partly out of respect for its founder, Alexander the Great.

Meanwhile the question arose: What to do with Antony's body, still entombed with his lover and her maids? Octavian allowed

Cleopatra to deploy the sophisticated burial practices for which the Egyptians were famous and bury her lover's corpse with the appropriate rites and splendor.

After Antony's funeral Cleopatra stopped eating and seemed intent on starving herself to death, but she was persuaded to end her fast when Octavian threatened the lives of her children. An element that stands out in these scenes, though little is made of it by Plutarch, is how hard Cleopatra worked in her final hours to protect her sons and her daughter.

It has often been noted that Cleopatra distinguished herself from her Ptolemaic ancestors by being the only one to learn the Egyptian language. But what sets her apart even more decisively was the ferocity with which, until the end of her life, she tried to preserve the lives of her offspring. Her forebears—her own father among them—had killed their children in order to safeguard their own power. But though Cleopatra had arranged the deaths of at least one and possibly two of her siblings, and gone to war against a third, her children were another matter.

If these last scenes in the life of Cleopatra were dramatic, her final confrontation with Octavian pitched the action over into melodrama. Octavian visited her in her tomb, allegedly to comfort her. One wonders why free access to the locked vault was now available, why Octavian was not subjected to the indignity of being hoisted up on a derrick, like the dying Antony. Nor was he excluded, like Proculeius, who had been obliged to sneak in through a window.

Octavian found the queen haggard, distraught, her hair and eyes wild. Her robes and jewels had been put away, and she wore only her tunic. Plutarch cannot get past his fascination with the doomed woman's still lovely body and the allure that endured despite the precipitous decline in her circumstances. Though her chest was bruised from the self-administered beating with which she atoned for her mistreatment of Antony, "her famous charm and the boldness of her beauty were not entirely extinguished." She argued her case, pleaded necessity, blamed Antony, begged for mercy. She handed over a list of her treasures, which after all were Octavian's most salient concern. When a servant revealed that she was hiding some of her jewels, she begged to be allowed to set aside a few last trinkets as gifts to send Octavian's wife and his sister, Octavia, Antony's wife.

Cleopatra and Octavian were both lying, but Cleopatra—who convinced Octavian that she wanted to live—appears to have been better at it. The suicide watch must have eased as she secretly continued with her plans to kill herself and be spared the humiliation of being exhibited among the trophies of Octavian's victory.

Cleopatra discovered that Octavian was about to leave for Syria and was planning to send her and her children to Rome. She begged to be allowed to perform one last funeral rite for Antony, and as she poured a final offering (most likely wine and honey) over his sarcophagus, she spoke—poetically and movingly—about the fact that though indivisible in life, they were now in danger of being parted forever. They would in death change places: she would be in Rome, and he would remain in Egypt.

She kissed Antony's coffin, then ordered her bath to be drawn. She dined well, lay down, and waited for the delivery from the countryside of a basket of figs. It was said that she ordered her maids to dress her as the goddess Isis. (Cleopatra's biographer Michael Grant has suggested that she may have been wearing a bit of jewelry or finery alluding to Isis's association with snakes, and that this may have been a source of the story of how Cleopatra died.)

She offered some of the figs to her guards, who instructed the messenger to bring in the basket. She sent a tablet that she had already written to Octavian, then ordered everyone to leave except her two maids, and shut the door.

The tablet was a suicide note, but when Octavian rushed his men to Cleopatra's rescue, it was already too late. She was dead. Her two maids, also poisoned, died immediately.

The basket of figs had concealed a venomous asp. Apparently it had been Cleopatra's hope that she would be bitten before she knew that it was happening, a detail reminiscent of Caesar's expressed wish for a quick, unexpected death. Seeing the snake, she is reported to have said, "So here it was, after all," and stretched out her arm.

Even the method of her suicide — the poisonous asp bite — has been debated. Thanks to Plutarch and Shakespeare, we "know" that Cleopatra had the deadly snake concealed in a basket of figs and smuggled into the tomb where she was hiding from the victorious Roman leader. But some experts have noted that the deadly Egyptian cobra was far too bulky, unruly, and menacing to be hidden in even the roomiest, most ingenious fruit basket. Toxicologists have argued that even if the venom proved deadly — which was not always or dependably the case — the victim would have taken hours to die, whereas Cleopatra's death has been reported, and dramatized, as having been instantaneous.

Attached forever to the snake, Cleopatra takes her place in that most romantic group: highly eroticized female suicides. From Sappho jumping from the cliff to Sylvia Plath kneeling at the oven door, Cleopatra outdoes them all for the high drama and the ghoulish sexiness of how she is said to have perished.

Plutarch provides a succession of variant explanations of how Cleopatra died. Some accounting must have seemed required to explain how a cobra had been smuggled past the guards, who would suffer if Cleopatra killed herself, as she had threatened to do. In one scenario, the asp arrived in a water jug from which Cleopatra had to tease and provoke it until it rose up and bit her. It is intriguing to imagine the Egyptian queen tempting the killer snake to emerge from the jug; in addition, it does seem like a clever way to transport a snake—in a heavy container with a narrow mouth or lid.

Plutarch also suggested that she hid the poison in a hollow hairpin. The Egyptians were known for their medical expertise, and poison may simply have been part of a doctor's toolkit. Cleopatra would not have needed to experiment on prisoners to find out what she could ask the soothsayers who flocked to her court or could discover among the volumes in the Alexandrian library.

After death, Cleopatra's body was found to be pure and uncorrupted, like the corpse of a saint. No bruises or dark patches indicated the effects of poison, though Octavian was informed that two puncture wounds showed the cause of death.

If Plutarch had his doubts about the murderous asp, Duane Roller lays out the reasons why the basket of figs and the romantic death by snakebite were unlikely to have happened. "The basket would have been very large (the Egyptian cobra is several feet in length) and . . . Cleopatra's guards would not likely have been asked to help themselves if an asp had been hidden in it. . . . There would have needed to be expert snake handlers on hand. The Egyptian cobra can be fatal, but only if its venom is injected into a vital spot; otherwise the victim is more likely to make a full recovery. . . . All evidence is that it would be a complex method of death with little certainty of success."

In a video interview, Andrew Gray, curator of herpetology at the Manchester Museum, brings the expertise of a scientist to the question of how Cleopatra died. An Egyptian cobra, often five or six feet long, could hardly have been transported in a basket of figs. More to the point, there was only a small chance that a person would die from a cobra bite. Most such bites were "dry" and only rarely involved an injection of venom. Even if she had been bitten, a full recovery was likely. Only 10 percent of snakebite wounds are fatal, and on the slim chance that this one was, the death would have been agonizing—as Cleopatra would have known. Finally, it was impossible for Cleopatra to pass the snake along to kill her two maids, because a cobra strikes only once.

But if she was not bitten by a snake, something else must have killed her. Yet like so much about her life and death, we will never know what that was.

Plutarch tells that the snake was never found inside the tomb. He adds a brief, haunting story about some witnesses who claimed to have seen from the window of the tomb, the winding trail that the serpent left in the riverbank as it slithered away from the scene of the crime. To say that someone saw from a high window the shallow groove dug in the sand by a serpent is an eloquent way of raising the question of whether the thing actually happened.

"But no one knows the truth," writes Plutarch.

Cleopatra's long and steady hold on our collective psyche might have been weaker and less enduring without the perverse romance of the (alleged) method of her suicide: so original, so brave, so dramatic. No other death could have so intrigued and delighted the generations of painters who represented her last moments as a bare-breasted orgasmic swoon.

In the Middle Ages, images of the Egyptian queen were relatively decorous. Rarely far from his prey, the snake is unlike the talking serpents we see in later art: the evil snake tempting Eve as it coils around the forbidden tree. This snake is an assassin, a hired killer, an agent of sudden death.

In the Boucicaut Master's miniature illustration for Boccaccio's *On Famous Women,* Antony and Cleopatra are lifeless, laid out side by side, a medieval king and queen carved in stone on a royal tomb. Both wear a crown and a robe. The scene is calm and stately; the only disruptive elements are the sword protruding from Antony's chest and the serpent encircling Cleopatra's bare forearm like a deadly bracelet. A woodcut illustrating a German translation of Boccaccio depicts Antony, here too impaled on a sword, as Cleopatra gazes mournfully at him, while a snake with odd pointy ears embeds its fangs in her arm.

Plutarch specifies that the snake was said to have bitten the queen on the arm. But by the late fifteenth century, the site of the wound has migrated to her breasts. In an illustration for yet another edition of Boccaccio, done in 1480 in Bruges, Cleopatra's ermine-trimmed red robe has slipped down around her hips. Not just one but two snakes are attached to her, one to each of her breasts.

What is remarkable is not only how often Cleopatra has been painted but how many of these images represent the Egyptian queen entirely nude or, more often, naked from the waist up, one or both breasts bared to receive the serpent's venom—a serpent smaller, quicker, and meaner than the Egyptian cobra. Her body is invariably creamy, plump, luscious, and notably pale. These works grew in popularity during the centuries of European expansion into Africa and Asia. The fascination with exoticism and the East was perfectly embodied in a beautiful dark-haired woman, preferably naked, ideally dying or dead.

In Giampietrino's painting *The Death of Cleopatra* (1504), the queen has removed all her clothes and turned her lovely head away from us. With one hand she raises the lid on a straw basket while the other presses the snake against her chest, its fangs so close to her nipple that it almost appears to be nursing. Later in the century, Michele Tosini dresses the queen in a pale pink gown that she pulls aside, baring her breast so that the snake can reach her pearlescent flesh. In Guido Reni's *Cleopatra* (1628) the snake has been shrunk to the size of a worm, but Cleopatra is massive, her broad shoulders, strong arms, and half-bared chest braced for the deadly strike. By the end of the seventeenth century, these images of Cleopatra and the serpent were so common that several appear in painted enamel on the faces of pocket watches.

Most of these Cleopatras are in the throes of rapture. With their heads thrown back, their eyes cast upward, the faces of these Egyptian queens resemble those of the female saints and martyrs or, closer to home, the painters' wives and mistresses in the midst of, or just after, sex.

In 1876, the American sculptor Edmonia Lewis created a very different image of the death of Cleopatra. She chose to portray the queen as Caucasian, though Lewis, who was Black, elsewhere represented Black women in her work. Her image of the dying monarch is neither eroticized, ecstatic, nor sensational. Fully clothed, regal, wearing a crown decorated with a serpent, seated on a throne that is adorned with two sphinx heads, she turns her head slightly to one side, her chin just barely uplifted, awaiting death with fortitude, dignity, and resolve.

Denied the opportunity to bring Cleopatra to Rome in captivity, Octavian, according to Suetonius, was so disappointed by her death that he ordered the Psylli, an African people famous for their knowledge of poisons, to try and reverse the effect of the venom. Their attempt was unsuccessful, and the efforts of the Psylli appear in none of the other classical sources.

Even without the trophy queen, Octavian had won. He ordered that Cleopatra be buried beside Antony with the rites and honors befitting her nobility of spirit. She died at thirty-nine, Antony at fifty-three.

Octavian made an official visit to pay his respects at the tomb of Alexander the Great, placing a golden crown on it and scattering it with flowers. But when he was asked if he wanted to see the tombs of the Ptolemies, he is supposed to have replied that he wanted to see a king—not dead bodies. Statues of Antony were destroyed, but a supporter of Cleopatra's is said to have paid Octavian to leave her statues in place, another indication of the role that money played in Rome's dealings with Egypt.

Antony and Fulvia's son, Antyllus, went into hiding but was betrayed by his tutor and subsequently beheaded. The tutor was in turn killed for having stolen the precious gem that Antyllus wore around his neck—a plot detail that conveys the chaos, desperation, and criminality of a society in which the teacher steals a valuable keepsake from the headless corpse of his pupil.

Caesarion fled to India but was tricked into returning when he was told that he would be crowned king. Upon his return he was killed, thus confirming Cleopatra's worst fears for her eldest son and suggesting that she may have failed to instill him with her gifts for perspicacity, strategy, and survival. Octavian is supposed to have said that the world only had room for one Caesar, and although Caesarion was raised to believe that he was that singular figure, common sense might have warned him that Octavian would disagree. Soon afterward, Octavian issued an edict proscribing images of Caesarion; a room in Pompeii that was decorated with a wall painting of Caesarion and his mother is said to have been walled off after Octavian's directive.

Except for Antyllus and Caesarion, the children that Antony

and Cleopatra had, separately and together, were sent to Rome to be raised by Octavia.

Octavia is one of the more impressive characters to have emerged from the pages of Plutarch: a woman raising five children, three of whom she inherited from the Egyptian queen for whom her second husband left her and for whom he was said to have died. By the end of her life, Octavia's brother, by then the emperor Augustus, had accorded her a position and honors rarely given Roman women.

In 23 BCE, her beloved son (and her brother's designated heir) Marcellus died of an illness ravaging Rome. In his *Life of Virgil*, Aelius Donatus describes Octavia fainting when Virgil recited aloud a line from his *Aeneid* (6. 884), a section in which Aeneas meets the ghost of Marcellus — still young, still beautiful — in the underworld. A beautiful neoclassical painting by Jean-Joseph Taillasson, *Virgil Reading the Aeneid to Augustus and Octavia* (1787), is a tender depiction of melancholy and grief. It is also a dramatization of an artist's shock on getting a reaction so wholly unlike whatever response he might have expected.

Plutarch tracks Cleopatra and Antony's offspring through generations, a seemingly rambling list of marriages and children, like the begats in the Old Testament, except that there is a punch line: Two descendants of Antony became emperor and both subsequently went insane, a fact that would seem to defy the laws of coincidence and of averages. One of these was Caligula, who killed his wife and child; the other, Nero, murdered his mother and nearly destroyed the Roman Empire. "He was fifth in descent from Antony," is how Plutarch ends the *Life of Antony*, seeming to relish the fact that Antony's lineage included two deranged and murderous emperors.

Alexander Helios lived long enough to participate with his twin sister, costumed as the sun and the moon, in Octavian's triumphal procession after his conquest of Egypt — the ceremonial march in which he had so desperately wanted to exhibit Cleopatra. The ceremony sounds very much like a cruel parody of the Donations of Alexandria. The children were paraded along with an image of their mother with an asp still clinging to her body. Aside from the pain it must have caused the orphaned twins, the image of the snake helped determine the narrative of how Cleopatra died.

Her two younger sons died young, in Rome, presumably of disease.

In 25 BCE, Cleopatra Selene, Cleopatra's daughter with Antony, the only one of her children to have survived childhood, was married at fifteen to Juba II, the son of Juba I, the late Numidian king. Like Cleopatra's three children, Juba II had also been raised by Octavia after his father's death. The newlywed couple were sent to Mauretania, in northwestern Africa. Octavian, now Emperor Augustus, wanted someone he could trust to take charge of this strategically important and commercially lucrative territory.

Together the royal couple transformed a quiet outpost into a vibrant metropolis, a city named Caesarea. Much as her mother had revitalized Alexandria, Cleopatra Selene oversaw building projects and supported education and the arts. She introduced the use of the Greek language, and attracted scholars, philosophers, and historians, who contributed to the cultural and intellectual life of the city. Himself a scholar, Juba II wrote learned histories of North Africa and Arabia.

At some point between 13 and 9, Cleopatra Selene gave birth to a son whom she named Ptolemy. She is believed to have died around that time, leaving Juba II to rule over Mauretania for thirty more years, until he was succeeded by Ptolemy, who appears to have inherited the weaker parts of his grandfather Antony's character. Self-indulgent and indecisive, he lasted until 40 CE, when he was executed by Caligula, presumably for the sin of having minted gold coins and otherwise exceeded the authorized limits of his official power.

The events that followed Cleopatra's death have made her accomplishments clear. However turbulent, the decades during which she remained in power contributed to her country's culture, security, and well-being. She marshaled her skills and powers to fend off the ambitions of Rome until her defeat marked a turning point, after which her powerful legend would long survive the diminution and demolition of much that she had achieved.

PART II

The Afterlife of Cleopatra

CHAPTER SEVEN

The Pearl

Antony's secretary, Lucius Munatius Plancus, is thought to be the source of a story later recounted in Pliny's *Natural History* — an anecdote that was considered to exemplify Cleopatra's reckless, theatrical decadence. Allegedly she wore as earrings two of the world's largest pearls. At the end of an especially sumptuous banquet, and in a competitive spirit brought on by the flirty question of which lover, Antony or Cleopatra, hosted more lavish feasts, she removed one of the pearls from her ear, dissolved it in vinegar (or wine) and offered it as a toast to Antony. He proceeded to drink it, aware or unaware that the dissolved pearl was supposedly an aphrodisiac.

Ultimately, the truth of this story (science tells us that pearls are not actually soluble in either wine or vinegar) matters less than its popularity and durability. Its significance lay in the role that it played in the Roman campaign to portray Cleopatra, during her lifetime and after her death, as the personification of Eastern licentiousness and dissolution. It was yet another exemplary fable about how the East needed the West to instill a conscience, a sense of order, a moral uprightness and self-respect in its population—a sense of restraint that, it was hoped, would counter distasteful Eastern stunts like dissolving the world's largest pearl in wine and offering it to one's lover.

True or not, the story has become one of the most well-known and frequently portrayed "incidents" in the life of Cleopatra. In a fifteenth-century woodcut illustrating the German translation of Boccaccio's *On Famous Women*, Antony and another guest watch Cleopatra drink from the cup in which she has liquefied the giant pearl.

A considerably more elaborate and heavily populated version of this story appears in several paintings by Tiepolo, believed to have been done around 1744. Seated at one end of a table covered with an embroidered white cloth, Cleopatra, dressed in the finery of eighteenth-century royalty, holds the pearl, pinched between her fingers. She is just about to drop it into the cup.

At the opposite end of the table, Antony, in a golden helmet and an improbably orange robe, sits back, watching intently. His surprise is echoed in the postures and faces of the courtiers and servants gathered around the table, avidly observing the wild excess and casual exhibitionism of the Egyptian queen. She has captured their full attention. Beneath the dais on which she sits, a man tries to control his horse, but he is among the very few not looking at Cleopatra. What is remarkable is how much drama Tiepolo extracts from a relatively static moment—a woman is dropping something into a cup—as well as the artist's assumptions about his culture and the milieu in which he lived; the painting's intended audience would have understood what they were being shown.

Tiepolo's vision is rather like a three-ring circus compared to Carlo Maratta's *Cleopatra*, painted four decades earlier. Cleopatra occupies nearly the whole canvas, on which there is only a woman,

a cup, and a pearl. The queen could not be more classically European—not remotely Egyptian, or even what we might imagine as
Greek: Northern Italian, perhaps. She is dressed like a goddess—
that is, like an extremely rich woman of Maratta's time—swathed
in gorgeous material, in dazzling colors, draped in heavy cloth embroidered with flowers and edged with gold brocade.

At the center of the canvas is the pearl. It is pear-shaped, as
long as Cleopatra's thumb and considerably thicker. It shines with
a wholly different light from that of anything else in the painting.
In Cleopatra's other hand is a heavy chalice with a handle that, like
the ribbon coiled on the queen's shoulder, resembles a snake.

In the late seventeenth century, Maratta was a popular painter,
with important patrons from the Roman aristocracy and higher
echelons of the church. Their Cleopatra was not precisely the greedy
monster that the ancient Romans imagined; for them, her display
of excessive wealth might have represented something aspirational.
She had to be foreign, indeed Eastern, in name if not in appearance
to enable their frank enjoyment of a beautiful, decadent woman,
richer even than they were and without whatever vague anxiety
they might have felt about their own costly tastes.

Though Plutarch's portrait of Cleopatra would turn out to be
more nuanced and sympathetic than perhaps he intended, it contained more than enough ammunition for later writers to use against
women in general, and Cleopatra in particular. Boccaccio found
her "truly notable for almost nothing, except her ancestry and beauty;
she was known throughout the world for her greed, cruelty, and
excess" (quoted in Jones). Antony's passion for the wicked monarch has been seen as a warning about how a hero can be ruined
by a real-life Eve or Circe, a scheming proto–Lady Macbeth.

Her sinful "desires" prompted Dante to send her to the second
circle of hell, where she was doomed to spend eternity among the

lustful. The Latin historian Sextus Aurelius Victor (fourth century CE) tells us that she prostituted herself in an effort to cool her burning sexual heat, and that she was "so beautiful that many men bought a night with her at the price of their lives" (quoted in Jones).

This last view of Cleopatra may have inspired Alexander Pushkin, whose unfinished story "Egyptian Nights" (1837) features an Italian who performs improvisations on topics suggested by his audience. Asked to invent a poem on the subject of Cleopatra and her lover, the actor creates a scenario in which the queen announces that her love is for sale, but at enormous cost. The lucky winner will pay with his life for one night in her bed. Three men—a gray-haired soldier, Flavius; a young philosopher named Kriton; and an even younger unnamed boy—volunteer to accept the fatal bargain. Cleopatra promises them each a night of "sensual fires" but reminds them that at dawn, "The deadly axe will fall upon / The heads of all my lucky ones." And no one seems to feel that the price is too steep to pay.

Her actual lovers Julius Caesar and Mark Antony appear to have been less important to Pushkin than what Cleopatra represented: sex worth dying for, and the cruelty and capriciousness—so supposedly female, so allegedly Eastern—to make death the cost of the bargain.

A similar dynamic propels in Théophile Gautier's story "One of Cleopatra's Nights," published in 1838. After catching her hopelessly besotted admirer, Meïamoun, spying on her in her bath, the queen agrees to host him for one night of love. She entertains him at a lavish banquet, at the end of which, at daybreak, she serves him a cup of poison. When Antony returns and inquires about the corpse, Cleopatra tells him that she was only testing the efficacy of the poison she intends to take if she is captured by Augustus, and she invites Antony to join her watching the Greek clowns dance.

A later story—perhaps apocryphal—has a Victorian audience member remarking that Queen Victoria's home life was surely very different from the intense suffering and the raging passion that Sarah Bernhardt portrayed when she played Cleopatra mourning Antony onstage. Lucy Snowe, the heroine of Charlotte Brontë's *Villette*, is troubled by a painting of the "larger than life" Cleopatra lounging on her sofa, dressed in clothes that fail to adequately cover her distressingly voluptuous body. Lucy's fiancé, Paul Emanuel, scolds her just for *looking* at the painting.

CHAPTER EIGHT

Shakespeare's Cleopatra

Without additional biographical information, an audience watching Shakespeare's *Antony and Cleopatra* might have a hard time understanding what exactly its nominal heroine did before she met Antony. We might well wonder what it would have meant to be queen of Egypt when Cleopatra seems to have no duties or responsibilities beyond her strenuous efforts to make sure that the flame of Antony's passion for her does not flicker or die out. It is yet another example of the way in which Cleopatra has been defined by her relationship with her lovers rather than by her own record, her own achievements and accomplishments.

Antony and Cleopatra (1607) may be one of Shakespeare's busiest and most chaotic plays. It has an enormous cast of characters, and for much of the action at least two things are happening in two different places. There is something disorienting about the frequent scene changes and shifts of locale, the reverses in what we feel for the characters and in what they seem to feel about one another. The semi-constant disruptions can make the drama seem oddly modern and experimental, less *King Lear* than the Wooster Group or Richard Foreman.

In a perceptive essay, "Shakespeare's Boy Cleopatra, the Decorum of Nature, and the Golden World of Poetry," Phyllis Rackin argues that the "recklessness" of the play's structure and its use of language — "a curious mixture of the most elevated Latinisms and the coarsest contemporary slang" — echo the behavior of its heroine.

> The episodic structure, with its multiplicity of tiny scenes ranging in setting from one end of the known world to the other, directly opposed the growing neoclassical demand for the Unities. . . . The bewildering parade of tiny, scattered scenes requires explanation, as does the diffusion of the catastrophe through the last two acts. . . . What is perhaps most reckless of all, and most offensive to neoclassical taste, is Shakespeare's presentation of his heroine, for his Egyptian queen repeatedly violates the rules of decorum. . . . Cleopatra's incredible parade of shifting moods and stratagems, together with Shakespeare's notorious reticence about her motives, has led even her admirers to conclude that her one salient quality is, paradoxically, her lack of one — the magnificent inconstancy that Enobarbus calls "infinite variety."

Those going to Shakespeare for a deeper or more complex understanding of the nature of Cleopatra might be wise to look elsewhere. Cleopatra is at once one of the most vocal, the most self-dramatizing, and ultimately the most opaque of Shakespeare's heroines.

The play contains astonishing flashes of gorgeous poetry (most of them given to Cleopatra) as well as dramatic moments that require great delicacy to avoid either underplaying or overdoing. Among these passages is the scene in which Cleopatra interrogates a messenger about Octavia. He says, a bit dismissively, that she is thirty, meaning that she is over the hill, and Cleopatra's reaction —

she herself is thirty-nine—has to be precisely right. There is an affecting scene in which Antony complains that Caesar sees him the way he is and not the way he used to be. This passage too requires a pitch-perfect delivery to awaken our deeper sympathies for the beleaguered hero.

The poet John Berryman tactfully called the play a "relaxation" from *Macbeth*, which Shakespeare wrote the previous year: "a relaxation affecting structure, versification, material and manner. There is no true development either upward or downward in the play. For 1,700 lines, up to the action at Actium, the hero's fortunes (and the heroine's) are at their height; then, after an interim of 35 lines wherein the woe is announced by others, for 1,300 lines their fortunes are at the bottom."

Berryman has done the mathematics for us, but we understand what he means. We do not feel, as we do in *Macbeth*, the rising tension between the inevitable and the unexpected, an inexorable and unstoppable force propelling the action forward. Here one thing happens, then another. The characters react. A war begins and ends and flares up again. The scene changes from Alexandria to Rome, then we hear the disturbing news about a series of battles. But the lovers never seem to be part of it; the serious drama is transpiring elsewhere, while they exist in a kind of bubble, enacting the theatrics of a dying love affair.

Brilliant direction would be required to work around the fact that, because of the way Shakespeare writes her part, the patient, steady, wronged-against Octavia is far more appealing and sympathetic than her Egyptian rival. Octavia does not ask as much of us, or of Antony, and she never grates on our nerves as Cleopatra more often does. Likewise, inspired stagecraft would be necessary to give the scene of the dying Antony being hoisted up to the tomb the pathos and horror it has in Plutarch. It is hard to envision a version of this turn in the narrative that wouldn't be more grotesque than tragic as we watch it transpire before us.

Shakespeare, as we know, borrowed his plot and most of the characters from Plutarch; some of his language was taken from Thomas North's 1579 English translation. Enobarbus's rhapsodic description of the golden barge in which Cleopatra sailed to meet Antony is essentially paraphrase, and the borrowing grows more direct as the play nears its end. Antony's last enjoinder to his men, that they eat, drink, and be merry because by tomorrow he may be dead and they will be serving another master, is quoted almost verbatim, though the "withered corpse" he fears becoming is transformed nicely into "a mangled shadow." Antony's somewhat sad last words, his valiant boast that he was "a Roman killed by a Roman" are the same in Plutarch and Shakespeare.

Shakespeare also seems to have followed the arc of Plutarch's gradual, even reluctant, warming toward the character of Cleopatra. In the play, the first words we hear about Cleopatra are *gypsy* and *strumpet* and the rest of the drama marks a gradual and uneven progression from these harsh offhand judgments to something closer to admiration for the queen, who only at the edge of death begins to seem, as Charlotte Brontë says in *Villette,* larger than life. Even then our sympathy for Cleopatra falls far short of the pity we feel for Lear or Juliet. We are never entirely on Cleopatra's side, and by the end we may find ourselves a little tired of her, exhausted by Antony and by their overheated accusations, complaints, misunderstandings, and reconciliations.

What is striking is what Shakespeare took from Plutarch, and what he chose to leave out: namely, anything that Cleopatra might have done outside the tomb and the bedroom. When in act 5 Cleopatra asks that Octavian give Egypt to her son, we may well wonder, "What son?" Caesarion has been mentioned, in passing, only once before.

Unlike Plutarch, Shakespeare had seen in his own lifetime that a woman was fully capable of running a country; his play was written not long after the death of Queen Elizabeth I. He could, had he chosen to do so, have departed from Plutarch to make the drama more closely resemble *Macbeth*, his most recent composition. With substantial revisions, it could have echoed *Macbeth*'s study of how a power-hungry woman urges her mate to get what he wants but cannot convince himself to go after. But Shakespeare's Cleopatra has none of the flinty tormented complexity of the Scottish chieftain's homicidal wife.

Shakespeare chose to draw from Plutarch the same conclusions that the classical writer wanted his readers to reach. Cleopatra existed largely to be Antony's serious mistake, though (at least near the end of her life) her story was as engaging as his. For all Cleopatra's electric energy and her lyrical speeches, Octavia is Shakespeare's true heroine-martyr: a decent woman exploited by her brother, her husband, and her husband's mistress.

Many writers on Shakespeare, Berryman among them, have noted that *Antony and Cleopatra* is more of a history play than a tragedy in that it follows the succession of "real" events rather than the rise and fall of a singular tragic fate. It dramatizes multiple meetings at which cabals are formed and dissolved, urgent plans and agreements made and broken, alliances arranged and altered. But unlike the great tragedies, it fails to make us feel the grief we experience at the death of Lear, Macbeth, and Hamlet. Macbeth is a murderer, Lear a foolish old man, and Hamlet an indecisive young one, and yet we overlook their flaws and mourn their loss. If we are expecting something similar to happen at the conclusion of *Antony and Cleopatra*, we may be disappointed; Shakespeare has not managed to overcome his ambivalence toward his hero and heroine, and this makes it harder for us to overcome our own mixed feelings.

If *Antony and Cleopatra* is indeed a history play, it is an unusual one, in that Cleopatra—one of the two main characters in the chronology it dramatizes—seems to have only a tangential role in its historical events. Though her political and military strategies were deciding factors in the war between Octavian and Antony, Shakespeare never lets us see the queen doing anything but flirting with Antony, suffering agonies of jealousy, flirting more, retreating to the tomb with orders that Antony be told she is dead, receiving Antony's body, mourning Antony, greeting the peasant with the fig basket, pressing the serpent to her breast, and dying. One cannot imagine this woman governing a kingdom or staving off the incursions of the Roman Empire for twenty years. How would she have found the time and energy for statecraft, administration, and diplomacy when so much of her attention was focused on her romantic rivals?

Before the play begins, Shakespeare's Antony is already destroyed. He has sacrificed his responsibilities, his notions of duty, and his sense of himself for Cleopatra. He has let himself be dominated by her, and the consequences have been as dire as Plutarch warned us that they would be. Yet we never see Shakespeare's Cleopatra as dominant so much as willful, lascivious, and seductive. She does not seem capable of (or interested in) steering Antony into a series of fatal errors, and when disaster strikes, and he accuses her of betraying him, we are not entirely sure why he holds her responsible. Something is off in the balance between the lovers and the world around them. We would have had to have read Plutarch to understand that a country and an empire are at stake for both of them. No matter who plays Shakespeare's Cleopatra—among the best was the brilliant Mark Rylance, who staged the play with an all-male cast, as it would have been staged in Shakespeare's time—the words *drama queen* may at some point cross the viewer's mind.

In her essay "Egyptian Queens and Male Reviewers," Linda T. Fitz critiques the way Cleopatra has been deprived of her individuality and turned into "the archetypal woman: practiser of feminine wiles, mysterious childlike, long on passion and short on intelligence—except for a sort of animal cunning." Fitz quotes a succession of male critics, commenting on Shakespeare's portrait of the Egyptian queen. Here is Harley Granville-Barker: "The passionate woman has a child's desires and a child's fears, an animal's wary distrust; balance of judgment none, one would say. But often. . . . she shows the shrewd skepticism of a child." And here is Edward Dowden: "At every moment we are necessarily aware of the gross, the mean, the disorderly womanhood in Cleopatra, no less than of the witchery and wonder which excite, and charm, and subdue" (in Steppat).

Fitz goes on to address the play's sexism, the double standard with which the behavior of Antony and Cleopatra is judged, the uncritical representation of the female fear of aging, the hatred of the sexuality that Cleopatra is taken to represent. We may feel that the truth is quite a bit more complicated, but we know what the writer means: the hatred for Cleopatra that has persisted through time, fed and mediated by the image of her as the ultimate seducer.

Our response to Cleopatra and her plight can depend on the particular production. In the 2017 BBC version, Antony tries to impale himself by falling with his sword on a bed, an inadvertently comical answer to the question of why the wound does not prove fatal. And in two productions I have seen, overly literal staging turns the scene of Antony's being hoisted up to his lover's tomb into something edging on farce.

There is one last beautiful speech that Shakespeare gives to Cleopatra, the passage in which she describes her dream of Antony, restored beyond the wreck he was at the end of his life, changed back to the man she fell in love with, only more divine and heroic in memory even than in life. It is a demanding one for an actress, this wounded cry of transcendent love exalted above the bickering, flirting, and jealous fits of the first four acts. Her passion and heartbreak are somehow intensified by the fact that she is constantly — and maddeningly — being interrupted by Dolabella, one of Octavian's agents.

Cleopatra: I dreamt there was an Emperor Antony.

      O, such another sleep, that I might see

      But such another man.

Dolabella: If it might please ye —

Cleopatra: His face was as the heav'ns, and therein stuck

      A sun and moon, which kept their course and lighted

      The little O, th'earth.

Dolabella: Most sovereign creature —

Cleopatra: His legs bestrid the ocean: his reared arm

      Crested the world: his voice was propertied

      As all the tuned spheres, and that to friends;

      But when he meant to quail and shake the orb,

      He was as rattling thunder. For his bounty,

      There was no winter in't: an autumn 'twas

      That grew more by reaping. His delights

      Were dolphin-like, they showed his back above

      The element they lived in.

That the man she describes bears only a passing resemblance to the one we have watched onstage only adds to the loneliness and the pathos of her loss; she is mourning someone whom she alone seems to have known and to remember.

Written seventy years later, John Dryden's introduction to his Antony and Cleopatra drama *All for Love* freely admits using Shakespeare and "the greatest wits of our nation" as a model. Like his predecessors, he was inspired by the "excellency of the moral: For the chief persons represented were famous patterns of unlawful love. . . . The crimes of love, which they both committed, were not occasioned by any necessity, or fatal ignorance, but were wholly voluntary; since our passions are, or ought to be, within our power, their end accordingly was unfortunate."

Understandably he worries that Octavia will draw all our sympathies away from Cleopatra—a flaw that does in fact prove a problem in Shakespeare's play, and that would remain difficult in later versions of Cleopatra's story, among them the 1963 film extravaganza: "Though I might use the privilege of a poet, to introduce [Octavia] into Alexandria, yet I had not enough considered, that the compassion she moved to herself and her children was destructive to that which I reserved for Antony and Cleopatra. . . . Though I justified Antony in some measure, by making Octavia's departure to proceed wholly from herself; yet the force of the first machine, like the cutting of a river into many channels, abated the strength of the natural stream." Dryden's solution to the problem does not entirely succeed: a confrontation between the two women that reduces our sympathy for them both.

Though its poetry never soars as high as Shakespeare's—passages do come close—Dryden's play is more tightly focused. It begins after Actium, when the couple are already defeated, and follows their downward trajectory. The action takes place over a single day, Antony's last. It avoids the dizzying shifts from Egypt to Rome and does not attempt to depict a turning point in history but rather focuses on the dramatic end of a catastrophic love affair: the sort of failed romance that levels everyone and everything in its path.

Dryden paid attention to the moments that stay with the reader from Plutarch — Dryden's own translation of Plutarch's *Lives* would appear five years later — and in a series of long scenes charts Antony's spiral into despair and Cleopatra's futile efforts to reanimate him with the will to live.

It is a pity that Dryden's play is not performed more often because it contains memorable moments that make the lovers seem more like human beings than the myths so familiar to us that nothing much can surprise us. There is, for example, a lovely exchange between the two while Antony lies dying:

Antony: But grieve not, while thou stayest,
My last disastrous times:
Think we have had a clear and glorious day,
And Heaven did kindly to delay the storm,
Just till our close of evening. Ten years' love,
And not a moment lost, but all improved
To the utmost joys — what ages have we lived!
And now to die each other's; and, so dying,
While hand in hand we walk in groves below,
Whole troops of lovers' ghosts shall flock about us,
And all the train be ours.
Cleopatra: Your words are like the notes of dying swans,
Too sweet to last. Were there so many hours
For your unkindness, and not one for love?

Shakespeare's Cleopatra

In the play's final lines, the priest Serapion delivers their eulogy:

> Sleep, blest pair,
> Secure from human chance, long ages out,
> While all the storms of fate fly oe'r your tomb,
> And fame to late posterity shall tell,
> No lovers lived so great, or died so well.

CHAPTER NINE

Cleopatra on Film

W as it accidental that the stage name of Theda Bara, who played the Egyptian queen in the 1917 film *Cleopatra*, is an anagram of *Arab Death?* Whether or not it was intentional, the studio made much of it as they created a fake identity for a young actress, transforming Theodosia Burr Goodman from Cincinnati into either an Arab or (in some versions) an Egyptian, the daughter of a Frenchwoman and either a sheikh or an Italian sculptor. The official story was that she had spent her childhood in Egypt in the shadow of the Sphinx. Sexy, exotic, Eastern, the girl from Cincinnati was referred to in the popular press as "the Serpent of the Nile."

The stills and sixteen seconds of film that remain and can be watched on YouTube are a perfect summation of the ways in which Cleopatra has been represented in visual art and on the screen: sly, sexy, exotic, half-naked. In a 1936 radio interview, Theda Bara, then fifty-one and retired from acting, described the "great fun" and challenge of making the film. The studio had no research department, and the actors had to find historical models for their own costumes. She claims to have worked with the curator of Egyptology at the Metropolitan Museum of Art, and it has been said that Bara, whose father was a tailor, cut the patterns herself.

Quite possibly the curator steered her away from the Egyptian collection toward the work of the orientalist painters, the lurid fantasies of Gérôme and Cabanel, the baroque ecstasies of Guercino. For Theda Bara's Cleopatra, *costume* meant almost no clothes. Her outfits vary from Asian-themed nightgowns to something a stripper might wear. With diaphanous cloths wrapped around her hips, minimal breast plates, and her skirts falling open to the thigh, she's a French painting gone pre–Production Code Hollywood. Among her more ornate articles of clothing is a skirt with a long train made entirely of peacock feathers.

In one of her most extravagant outfits, Bara is naked from the waist up except for two circular metal cages, like two coiled serpents, each wound around one of her breasts. These elaborate Art Deco adornments are attached to her shoulders by golden chains.

We can assume that the filmmakers had little interest in what the historical Cleopatra wore when she signed tax exemptions or met with the architects rebuilding Alexandria. Like the Cleopatra played by Vivien Leigh almost thirty years later, Theda Bara's queen is feline, but less a kittenish nymphet than a burlesque sex symbol. Her vampish makeup recalls the famous photo of Colette sitting with her legs crossed and cat whiskers drawn on her cheeks.

Of course the producers calculated that sex and a practically naked woman would sell more tickets than a film about a woman making decisions about irrigation projects. The problem again is not the focus on Cleopatra's love affairs but that the *sole* focus is on her love affairs. One wonders what the message was for young women at the start of the First World War: if you want to be famous, or immortal, find the richest, most powerful men and wear a transparent sarong and golden snakes on your breasts. And what did the film say to men? Women, especially Eastern women, were scheming, heartless, deceitful, and half-crazed with lust and sin.

The Theda Bara film has been said to have been at least partly inspired by H. Rider Haggard's novel *Cleopatra*. With its antiquated language, its faux-archaic diction, the 1889 novel seems oddly modern, only because the prose style and the plot conventions of its genre — the exotic adventure fantasy — have not changed much over the intervening years. Ideally, the racist exoticism of Haggard's work (most famously *King Solomon's Mines,* which inspired several sequels and films) has by now been largely excised from the genre, but you can open Haggard's novel at random and find a passage that would not seem out of place in a newly published romance.

Here is how the book begins:

By Osiris, who sleeps at Abouthis, I write the truth.

I, Harmachis, Hereditary Priest of the Temple, reared by the divine Sethi, aforetime a Pharaoh of Egypt, and now justified in Osiris and ruling in Amenti. I, Harmachis, by right Divine and by true descent of the blood King of the Double Crown, and Pharaoh of the Upper and Lower Land. I, Harmachis, who cast aside the opening flower of our hope, who turned from the glorious path, who forgot the voice of God in hearkening to the voice of a woman, I, Harmachis, the fallen, in whom are gathered up all woes as waters are gathered in a desert well, who have tasted of every shame, who through betrayal have betrayed, who in losing the glory that is here have lost the glory which is to be, who am utterly undone — I write, and by Him who sleeps at Abouthis, I write the truth.

Our narrator is a priest who has been ordered to drive Cleopatra and the Romans out of Egypt and restore the land to its true glory. Disguised as a physician, Harmachis is with Cleopatra in her final hours and poisons her, watering her poison and hoping she won't recognize him until he reveals his identity.

> "What's this?" she cried; "I grow cold, but I die not! Thou dark physician, thou has betrayed me!"
>
> "Peace, Cleopatra! Presently shalt thou die and know the fury of the Gods! *The curse of Menkau-ra hath fallen!* It is finished! Look upon me, woman! Look at this marred face, this twisted form, this living mass of sorrow! *Look! look!* Who am I?"
>
> She stared upon me wildly.
>
> "Oh! oh!" she shrieked, throwing up her arms; "at last I know thee! By the Gods, thou art Harmachis! — Harmachis risen from the dead!"

In the novel, Cleopatra's crime is that she has betrayed the temple priest for Mark Antony — and sold out Egypt to Rome. Haggard's novel was meant to be entertaining, as I suppose it was for readers whose enjoyed extremely bad writing plus Eastern cruelty plus operatic Asiatic passion.

Why should the two Hollywood films about Cleopatra — Cecil B. DeMille's 1934 epic starring Claudette Colbert and the 1963 extravaganza with Elizabeth Taylor in the title role — be so much more upsetting than Boccaccio calling Cleopatra "truly notable for almost nothing, except her ancestry and beauty; she was known throughout the world for her greed, cruelty, and excess"? Perhaps because the films are closer to us in time, and we feel more responsible; perhaps because it takes so much longer to watch the films (the 1963 film is four and a half hours long) than to read Boccaccio's brief damning sentences, so our investment is greater. Perhaps it was because Boccaccio was a better artist then the people responsible for the films. Or perhaps it is because the 1963 film was said to have been the most expensive movie ever made. So much money squandered on such a flawed production! It would be naive to complain that the films continue the long tradition of fixating on Cleopatra's romantic life rather than her political and public one. In fact both screenplays feature battles, an assassination, and a historic public procession, but Cleopatra is, once again, more of a bystander than a ruler.

As "the cunning Queen of the Nile," Claudette Colbert wields her beauty like a weapon. Playful, seductive, insinuating, she lures Roman leaders Julius Caesar (Warren William) and Mark Antony (Henry Wilcoxon) into her web. Though the film begins with a claim that it is based on "historical sources," no source as far as I know exists for its opening scenes.

First we see Cleopatra's maids bringing a sumptuous feast to her boudoir, only to find that she has vanished. She has been kidnapped, thrown into a speeding chariot, taken out to the desert, tied to a post, and left to die—like the damsel in the Victorian melodrama, bound to the train tracks by the mustachioed villain.

The kidnapping is her brother's doing. Young Ptolemy XIII is back in Alexandria with Caesar, who is about to sign a decree making Ptolemy the sole ruler of Egypt. Can nothing be done to stop him? Her predicament gives Cleopatra an excellent reason to dream up the stunt of being rolled up in the carpet, smuggled back into the city, and dropped at Caesar's feet.

But the brilliance of her plan pales beside the outfit that she has chosen for her journey in the rug: a low-slung skirt, open to the thigh, and a silken scarf wound around her neck, half covering her breasts. What is striking is not just that she is as naked as Theda Bara, as fetchingly nude as the women in the orientalist paintings. It is that the drape of the cloth and the way it follows her curves reminds us that clothing can be much more suggestive than bare flesh.

As the scene progresses, Cleopatra delivers one awful, cringeworthy line after another:

"Women should be toys for the great—it becomes them both."

"I'm no longer a queen, I'm a woman."

"Pothinus absconded with me to the desert and left me there to die. But nothing could stop me from greeting you."

"It seems strange to see you working. I've always pictured you either fighting . . . or loving."

The film goes out of its way to display—and sensationalize—the profligacy and decadence of which Cleopatra has been accused. The film appeared at one of the low points of the Great Depression. Nineteen thirty-four was also the year Adolf Hitler declared himself head of the German state. The splendor of the Egyptian court, presided over by a Ptolemaic sex goddess, was surely intended to provide distraction from the country's current and impending troubles.

Dissolving a giant pearl in a glass of wine would have seemed like a sad little party trick compared to the show Cleopatra stages within moments of luring Antony onto her barge. A bevy of dancing girls wriggle along the floor, each holding a large clam shell heaped with pearls and jewels. In an ecstasy of pride and orgiastic generosity, Antony and Cleopatra scoop jewels from the clam shells and fling them at a crowd scrambling to grab the loot until they are driven back by Egyptian officials with whips. Eventually, the riot morphs into a dance scene featuring women writhing in revealing leopard-skin costumes.

If each version of Cleopatra's life reflects the era in which it was created, the vehicles for Theda Bara and Claudette Colbert illustrate the twentieth century's discovery of the extent to which sex can sell a product. Of course this was nothing new. Cabanel and the other orientalist painters understood that the wealthy collector would feel more comfortable buying a canvas of a half-naked beautiful woman if she had a royal lineage: a historical figure with an exoticized background in the classics. But only in the twentieth century did Hollywood realize how profitable it could be: a passionate woman seducing two of antiquities' most famous and powerful men.

Starting with Cleopatra being kidnapped and left to die in the desert, the DeMille film has a casual relation to the facts. Its most elaborate scene is one that historians are fairly sure did not happen: the triumphal procession announcing Cleopatra's arrival to see Julius Caesar in Rome. It is widely agreed that both Caesar and Cleopatra had every reason for wanting to keep her visit to Rome quiet and avoid a spectacular show. But in the film we watch Cleopatra follow her lover in the riotous, heavily populated parade, regally enthroned on a float decorated with hawks and other symbols of Hollywood Deco Egypt.

At the end of the film, the snake bites Cleopatra in the breast, but it is done very tastefully and discreetly. The queen's hands are decorously positioned to hide the fangs sinking into her flesh. Even after death she manages to remain not only upright but regal: our final glimpse of her, enthroned against an elaborate backdrop, recalls almost precisely the pride and dignity with which she presided over her triumphal entry into Rome.

Perhaps the only thing that can be said for the film, in contrast to other cinematic versions of Cleopatra's story, is that it avoids the appalling racist caricatures found in the 1945 *Caesar and Cleopatra* and in the 1963 *Cleopatra*. In fact no actors of color appear to have been cast, though there is one distressing scene in which Caesar's wife, Calpurnia, tells her Roman girlfriend that her husband is in Egypt with his new mistress. It is all very giggly and feminine. The women are trying to figure out what Cleopatra looks like — that is, how serious a rival she is. It never occurs to them that anything would matter to a man except a woman's beauty.

"Is she Black?" asks one of the women, and they dissolve in laughter. Why do these Roman women think the idea is so hilarious? Calpurnia and her friends are white and blond, their hair meticulously and tightly waved in the fashion of Hollywood thirties starlets. Cleopatra is no less white, but her black hair and tipped-up eyeliner is intended to signal something more . . . Asiatic.

The life of Cleopatra has again been transformed into a crowd-pleasing orientalist fantasy. For the price of a ticket, American movie-goers could go into a theater and let Cleopatra's problems distract them from their own.

Many stories — some clearly true, some probably apocryphal — surround the making of the 1963 film now popularly known as the "Elizabeth Taylor *Cleopatra*." One anecdote concerns the first time Taylor actually watched the whole film on a screen — and vomited.

Even the film's admirers can sympathize with Taylor's response. Throughout much of the filming, she suffered from a series of serious illnesses and was repeatedly hospitalized. A severe bout of pneumonia required an emergency tracheotomy. On set, the married actress fell in love with her married co-star, Richard Burton. From the start, the Taylor-Burton love affair was tempestuous, allegedly marred by drunken violence.

And it's quite simply a terrible film. Taylor is called upon to deliver lines that not even the greatest actor could say with a straight face — and it's her job to make us believe them.

The film's inordinate length is only one manifestation of its peculiar sense of its own grandeur and importance. It opens with a still shot of a closed theater curtain and a sign that announces the "Overture." This lasts for two minutes and thirty-five seconds while quasi-Eastern orchestral music, cymbals twinkling and violins sobbing, play as we stare at the curtain.

The film begins with the aftermath of the Battle of Pharsalia. Military encampments dot the panoramic landscape along with pyres burning the corpses of those who have just been killed in Caesar's war with Pompey. Rex Harrison delivers the opening line, "The smoke of burning Roman dead is just as black and the stink no less." His entry into Alexandria, by boat, is elaborate. The Sphinx has been moved from the desert to the pier where the Roman ship docks. Pretending that they have come to shop at a farmers market on the palace steps, Julius Caesar is idly wandering about when the young pharaoh and his retinue appear.

Our awareness of the distance that we have traveled in the seventy years since the film was made comes with our first glimpse of the Black slaves bearing the litter on which Ptolemy rides. Their eyes are staring and vacant, their costumes pornographically skimpy, with elaborate loincloth pouches barely covering their genitals. Our unease is intensified by the film's portrayal of Pothinus, Ptolemy's "chief eunuch" — lisping, mincing, made up like a geisha. In case we still don't get it, Caesar makes a eunuch joke: "Chief eunuch — an exalted rank, taken not without a certain . . . shall we say . . . sacrifice?"

Among the most bizarrely entertaining books written about Cleopatra is *My Life with Cleopatra: The Making of a Hollywood Classic,* by Walter Wanger, the film's producer. An account of the nonstop crises that accompanied the making of the epic, the memoir reads like a cross between a film-set diary and the book of Job. Wanger describes a protracted horror show of costly mistakes, recalculations, revisions, wildly expensive setbacks. When Taylor insisted on being paid a million dollars, the studio proposed long lists of cheaper actresses, among them Joan Collins.

Considerable animosity was generated by the choice of the famous Hollywood hairdresser on whom Taylor insisted, a decision that enraged the British hairdressers' union. The hem of Taylor's ostrich-fringed gown caught fire, ignited by matches dropped on the floor. There were multiple changes of location, two directors, writers fired and hired; Lawrence Durrell was engaged to make the characters more nuanced. The insurance company kept insisting that the producers hire another actress to replace the ailing Taylor.

At one point, the production was sued for a hundred thousand dollars by an elephant wrangler who claimed that the company had insulted his elephants by describing them as "wild." Replacement elephants were imported from the United Kingdom. The handmaidens and slave girls went on strike, claiming that their costumes were too revealing; it is hard to imagine outfits skimpier than the ones that made it onto the screen.

And all the while the budget kept going up, topping out (it was said) at $44 million, around $400 million in "today's money." The construction of the London set required, wrote Wanger, "142 miles of tubular steel; enough RR ties for four miles of track; 20,000 cubic feet of timber; seven tons of nails; 300 gallons of paint—in short, *enough construction material for a development of about forty houses*" (emphasis mine). Palm trees were imported from Holland. Cleopatra's palace at Alexandria covered twenty acres. Its interior was almost as large and twice as high as Grand Central Station. Each major escalation in the budget necessitated meetings and fights and power shifts. Bad weather hampered the production, appropriately for a film set during an era in which everything depended on the flooding of the Nile.

Repeatedly Wanger explains why Cleopatra's story was worth

telling. "The whole canvas of this great world, with four dynamic personalities fighting for its domination . . . would appeal to every female in the world from eight to ninety. . . . It can be the last word in *opulence* [emphasis mine, again], beauty, and art — a picture women will love for its beauty and story. After all, it is the story of a woman who almost ruled the world but was destroyed by love."

The story of a woman who almost ruled the world but was destroyed by love. It was also the story of a woman who ruled Egypt for twenty years but was destroyed by the Roman Empire. But that is not the story that Wanger and his colleagues are telling.

It was a "women's picture" that promised to earn back the fortune spent on its creation. The film appeared in the same year as Betty Friedan's *The Feminine Mystique,* the best seller that suggested that women might want more than children, housework, and the thanks of the local PTA. Possibly for the first time, Cleopatra was seen as a heroic figure, with power, children, love, sexual freedom, amazing real estate, and money. The film offered viewers a fantasy beyond that purveyed by Claudette Colbert and Theda Bara. It made the audience want to *be* the Egyptian queen with her passionate lovers and fabulous clothes — and despite her harrowing ending. Its producers knew that it was the kind of film that could burnish a career and turn a profit that would silence the critics who had said it could never work.

We are twenty minutes into the film before Cleopatra appears — rolled up in a carpet. Inexplicably, Caesar seems to know what the carpet contains. In a weirdly sexualized moment Caesar asks why Apollodorus has put the rug down on the floor a certain way, and is told that it has been placed with the front side up. Caesar (by now holding a sword that he keeps playfully threatening to plunge into the carpet) insists that it be turned over. When inspecting a piece of merchandise, he says, I always like to look at its backside.

He flips the rolled-up carpet. And that's how the queen of Egypt emerges, tumbling onto the floor, face down, backside up.

More modestly dressed than her Hollywood predecessors, she shows that she has a brain by critiquing Caesar's maps. Soon after, Caesar's men have to tell him about the Egyptian queen, presumably because a Roman leader would have been incurious about the ruler of a country in whose affairs he was about to meddle.

The account of Cleopatra follows Plutarch—up to a point. "Reputed to be extremely intelligent and sharp of wit, Queen Cleopatra is widely read and considered to be well versed in the natural sciences and mathematics. She speaks seven languages." The lines about that intelligence outshining her beauty are omitted. This is Elizabeth Taylor, and nothing outshines her beauty. Nor do we find in Plutarch the casually misogynistic aside that Caesar lets slip: "Were she not a woman, one would consider her an intellectual."

Another crony adds additional details that might be "more interesting": "In obtaining her objectives, Cleopatra has been known to employ torture, poison, even her own sexual talents . . . which are . . . said to be considerable." (No transcription can convey the lewd spin that the actor gives these last words.) "Her lovers are listed more by number than by name. It's said that she chooses in the manner of a man rather than waiting to be chosen in a more womanly fashion." The listing of the lovers by number is an odd fact about a historical figure who as far as we know had only two.

This is followed by a scene in which Cleopatra is getting a full-body massage in the nude. Caesar forces his way into the chamber of half-naked women, and Cleopatra outlines her military situation while covering herself with a semi-transparent veil. She's radiating sex but more than that: she scolds Caesar for accidentally burning the Library of Alexandria. (A scholar who has been giving Cleopatra a lesson on epilepsy bemoans what has been lost in the blaze: "Aristotle's manuscripts, the histories, the Testament of the Hebrew God.") The saucy queen comes to the fiery defense of intellectual freedom. "How dare you and the rest of your barbarians set fire to my library. Neither you nor any other barbarian has the right to destroy one human thought."

What follows is one of those fierce cerebral arguments that in Hollywood films of certain eras function as foreplay. Snuggling against Caesar, Cleopatra murmurs, "Are you free to do whatever you want whenever you want?" And that's that. What else could she possibly mean?

Some effort is made to give us a sense of a mind existing within that irresistible body. Indeed this Cleopatra is something of a literary critic. "I've been reading your commentaries about your campaign in Gaul," she tells Caesar, flirtatiously. "Perhaps there's a little too much description."

The flirtation progresses. Caesar declares, "I have no son. . . . It is well known that Calpurnia is barren." To which Cleopatra replies, "A woman who cannot have children is like a river that has run dry," a situation she promptly remedies by bearing his son and instructing her maids to bring the baby to Caesar. If he picks up the child, it means he is acknowledging his rightful heir. Despite what history tells us about Caesar's refusal to acknowledge Caesarion, Caesar not only moons over the baby, but declares, at the top of his lungs, "I have a son!"

Inspired by the triumphal procession in the 1938 film, the producers fixated on a similar scene, staged on a much grander scale, to serve as the film's centerpiece. Once again, the fact that the procession could never have happened was of no import; the filmmakers hired six thousand extras and a large menagerie. The choreographer Hermes Pan was brought in to stage the parade. Recalls Wanger: "A Negro ballet is on one of the sound stages rehearsing;

athletes are practicing pole vaulting and sword play in the athletic field, with archers shooting nearby; the charioteers . . . are working out on one of the outdoor sets."

The assassination of Julius Caesar is portrayed as Cleopatra's personal tragedy. Though history has him at home in bed with the dreaming Calpurnia on the night before his death, waking to the sound of the doors and windows blowing open, Hollywood sends him on a stolen nocturnal visit to Cleopatra. He recites a list of troubling omens. Terrified, the Egyptian queen can only murmur, "I feel that you need me now, and I cannot help you."

After his murder Cleopatra flees Rome. Mark Antony helps her onto her gilded boat. Wearing a low-cut robe, she cries out in rage when she hears that Caesar has named Octavian as his heir rather than her own son. Again ignoring history, Antony offers to present Caesarion's claim to legitimacy to the Senate.

Antony inherits the power from the assassinated leader. When a crowd of boisterous soldiers crowns him with a laurel wreath, shouting and beating their shields with their swords in perfect unison, viewers may be reminded of similar scenes in Leni Riefenstahl's *Triumph of the Will*. The military association recurs a while later: the barge on which Cleopatra goes to meet Antony at Tarsus is the size of a modern naval aircraft carrier.

But first Cleopatra refuses to attend the meeting at Tarsus, a forceful response blunted by the fact that she delivers her answer naked, in the bath, while playing with a toy boat, a miniature golden barge. The scenes of their meeting last for some time: first a sumptuous banquet, then a long and seductive conversation during which Antony gets extremely drunk. Dancing girls in bikinis, their bare flesh gleaming with oil, put on a kind of sex show, featuring a float on which an actor dressed as Bacchus (plump and naked but for a gilded fig leaf) embraces a writhing woman dressed like Cleopatra. In his stupor, Antony stumbles across the floor, falling into the dancers, throwing Bacchus aside and practically assaulting the Cleopatra look-alike until he is let in on the joke.

He searches for Cleopatra, who is waiting for him in bed, inside a filmy canopy curtain that he — unable to part it — slices open with his sword. Later, when Cleopatra learns of Antony's marriage to Octavia, she takes her sword to her closet, destroys her boudoir, and stabs her bed multiple times, then bursts into tears.

The lovers' reconciliation is somehow connected to the Battle of Actium. Against his better judgment, Antony accedes to Cleopatra's insistence that they fight on the water. It is not clear whether the Egyptian queen knows best, or whether she is punishing him for his marriage to Octavia, or whether — this seems likeliest — she is testing his masculinity. In any case, he fails the test. Cleopatra is running this war.

But the male still has a few tricks up his sleeve. During an argument, Cleopatra slaps Antony, then slaps him again. He knocks her to the ground, where she remains and plays the rest of the scene looking up at him.

Cleopatra bids good-bye to Caesarion, who seems to be about twelve though we know that he was closer to eighteen. When he says that he is frightened, his mother replies, "All kings and especially queens are afraid, they just manage not to show it, something ordinary people cannot do." Especially queens?

Antony's death could not be clumsier or more awkwardly done; the wounded man is hoisted up to the window on a sort of woven stretcher. The lovers bid their tender good-byes. Cleopatra meets with Octavian, who repeats his desire to bring her as a victory trophy to Rome. He leaves, having exacted a promise that Cleopatra will do what he says. A basket is brought in. When we peer inside it, something wriggles. Cleopatra plunges in her hand, having first written to Octavian that her last wish is to be buried beside Antony. She muses that her life has been like someone else's dream, but now she will be in a dream of her own.

The final words we hear her say are, "Antony! Wait."

What might the historical Cleopatra have made of the representations of her over the two thousand years that have followed her death? How long would it have taken her to grasp first the concept of film, then the specifics of the 1938 pre-Code exploitation film or the hyper-serious 1963 epic — both supposedly about her? One thinks of a story told by Paul Bowles about the panic and shock of the Moroccan writer Mohammed Mrabet who saw the Charlton Heston film of *The Ten Commandments* and raced to tell Bowles the news that Cairo had been destroyed. (As it happens, Heston also made a film of Shakespeare's *Antony and Cleopatra* with Hildegarde Neil as Cleopatra, but it had limited release in the United States and generally poor reviews.)

What would she have thought about how she appeared on the page and on-screen — the ever changing balance of truth, exaggerations, and lies? As little as we know about her, one thing that seems clear is that she was not a person who shrank from the public view, nor from the work and danger of seizing and holding on to enormous political power. She was not a woman who avoided the spotlight, so would it have pleased her that after so much time that bright light was still shining? What would she recognize of herself in Elizabeth Taylor or Theda Bara, or in Plutarch or in Shakespeare?

Plutarch tells us that she was intelligent. For two dramatic and difficult decades she maintained the integrity and independence of an ancient civilization, for the last time until the twentieth century restored her country to itself. Perhaps she would understand how she has been seen from different angles, used to prove opposing political views, held up as a mirror for each era, as a screen on which to project changing and unchanging ideas about women, about empire, about power, and about the East.

Certainly it would be clear to her that she has not been forgotten, that the story of her life — and the misreadings, lies, and fantasies that augmented the facts — has changed and shifted over time, lodging her indelibly in our history and in the consciousness of our species.

Chronology

All dates BCE.

ca. 69	Cleopatra born in Alexandria
51	Cleopatra becomes co-ruler with her brother Ptolemy XIII
50	Ptolemy drives Cleopatra out of Egypt
48	Returning to Egypt, Cleopatra is defeated at Pelusium
	Pompey, defeated by Julius Caesar, is killed by Ptolemy XIII
48–47	Caesar supports Cleopatra; they defeat and kill Ptolemy XIII
	Cleopatra marries her brother Ptolemy XIV
	Cleopatra takes the throne and bears Caesar's son, Caesarion
46	Cleopatra, Caesarion, and Ptolemy XIV visit Rome as Caesar's guests
44	Caesar assassinated; Cleopatra and her family flee Rome for Alexandria
	Death of Ptolemy XIV
43	Cleopatra supports Octavian and Mark Antony against Caesar's assassins
42–41	Mark Antony meets with Cleopatra in Tarsus, returns with her to Alexandria
40	Birth of twins to Cleopatra and Antony; Antony returns to Rome, marries Octavia
37	Cleopatra gives financial support to Antony's Parthian campaign
34	Antony and Cleopatra preside over the Donations of Alexandria, celebrating their dynasty
	Split between Octavian and Antony
31	Battle of Actium; Antony and Cleopatra flee by ship from the battle
30	August: Suicides of Antony and Cleopatra in Alexandria

Genealogy

Ptolemy XII — Cleopatra V

Arsinoe IV   Berenice IV   Ptolemy XIII   Ptolemy XIV

Julius Caesar — Cleopatra VII — Mark Antony

Caesarion

Alexander Helios   Ptolemy Philadelphus

Cleopatra Selene — Juba II

Ptolemy

Bibliography

ANCIENT SOURCES

Caesar, Julius. *The Civil War: With Anonymous Alexandrian, African, and Spanish Wars*. Trans. John Carter. New York: Oxford University Press, 1997.

Cassius Dio. *See* Dio Cassius.

Cicero, Marcus Tullius. *The Letters of Cicero*. Vol. 4. Trans. Evelyn S. Shuckburgh. Althenmünster: Jazzybee Verlag Jürgen Beck, n.d.

Dio Cassius [Cassius Dio]. *Roman History*. Vol. 4: *Books 41–45*. Trans. Earnest Cary and Herbert B. Foster. Loeb Classical Library 66. Cambridge: Harvard University Press, 1916; Vol. 6: *Books 51–55*. Trans. Earnest Cary. Loeb Classical Library 83. Cambridge: Harvard University Press, 1917.

Diodorus Siculus. *Library of History*. Vol. 1: *Books 1–2.34*. Trans. C. H. Oldfather. Loeb Classical Library 279. Cambridge: Harvard University Press, 1933; Vol. 8: *Books 16.66–17*. Trans. C. Bradford Welles. Loeb Classical Library 422. Cambridge: Harvard University Press, 1963.

Hirtius, Aulus. *The Alexandrian War*. *See* Caesar, Julius.

Horace. *See* Thornton, William Thomas.

Jones, Prudence J. *Cleopatra: A Sourcebook*. Norman: University of Oklahoma Press, 2006.

Lucan, *The Civil War* (*Pharsalia*). Trans. A. S. Kline. Poetry in Translation, https://www.poetryintranslation.com/klineaslucan.php.

Lucian. *Icaromenippus; or, The Sky-man*. In Lucian, *The Downward Journey; or, The Tyrant. Zeus Catechized. Zeus Rants. The Dream; or, The Cock. Prometheus. Icaromenippus; or, The Sky-man. Timon; or, The Misanthrope. Charon; or, The Inspectors. Philosophies for Sale*. Trans. A. M. Harmon. Loeb Classical Library 54. Cambridge: Harvard University Press, 1915.

Plutarch. *The Age of Caesar: Five Roman Lives*. Trans. Pamela Mensch. Ed. James Romm. New York: Norton, 2017.

Plutarch. *Life of Antony*. Ed. C. B. R. Pelling. Cambridge: Cambridge University Press, 1988.

Bibliography

Plutarch. *The Lives of the Noble Grecians and Romans.* Trans. John Dryden. New York: Modern Library, 1932.

Propertius. *The Elegies.* Book 3. Trans. A. S. Kline. Poetry in Translation, https://www .poetryintranslation.com/PITBR/Latin/PropertiusBkThree.php#anchor _Toc201112466.

Strabo. *Geography.* Vol. 8: *Book 17, General Index.* Trans. Horace Leonard Jones. Loeb Classical Library 267. Cambridge: Harvard University Press, 1932.

Suetonius, *Lives of the Caesars.* Trans. Catherine Edward. New York: Oxford University Press, 2000.

Thornton, William Thomas. *Word for Word from Horace: The Odes Literally Versified.* London: Macmillan, 1878.

MODERN SOURCES

Beard, Mary, and Michael Crawford. *Rome in the Late Republic.* London: Duckworth, 1999.

Berryman, John. "The End." In *Berryman's Shakespeare.* Ed. John Haffenden. New York: Farrar, Straus and Giroux, 2000.

Boccaccio, Giovanni. *On Famous Women.* Trans. Guido A. Guarino. New Brunswick, N.J.: Rutgers University Press, 1963.

Canfora, Luciano. *The Vanished Library: A Wonder of the Ancient World.* Trans. Martin Ryle. Los Angeles: University of California Press, 1987.

Chauveau, Michel. *Cleopatra: Beyond the Myth.* Trans. David Lorton. Ithaca: Cornell University Press, 2002.

——. *Egypt in the Age of Cleopatra.* Trans. David Lorton. Ithaca: Cornell University Press, 2000.

Dell, Pamela. *Hatshepsut: Egypt's First Female Pharaoh.* Minneapolis: Compass Point Books, 2009.

Drakakis, John. *Antony and Cleopatra.* London: Macmillan, 1994.

Dryden, John. *All for Love: The World Well Lost.* Whitefish, Mont.: Kessinger, 2017.

Fielding, Sarah. *The Lives of Cleopatra and Octavia.* Ed. Christopher D. Johnson. Lewisburg, Pa.: Bucknell University Press, 1994.

Fitz, L. T. "Egyptian Queens and Male Reviewers: Sexist Attitudes in *Antony and Cleopatra* Criticism." *Shakespeare Quarterly* 28, no. 3 (Summer 1977): 297–316.

Gautier, Théophile. "One of Cleopatra's Nights." In Gautier, *One of Cleopatra's Nights and Other Fantastic Romances.* Trans. Lafcadio Hearn. New York: Hagemann, 1894.

Bibliography

Grant, Michael. *Cleopatra*. Edison, N.J.: Castle, 2004.

Granville-Barker, Harley. *Prefaces to Shakespeare*. Vol. 3: *Antony and Cleopatra, Coriolanus*. New Delhi: Atlantic, 2007.

Gruen, Erich S. "Cleopatra in Rome: Facts and Fantasies." In Miles, *Cleopatra*, 37–53.

Haggard, H. Rider. *Cleopatra*. Floating Press, 2012.

Hamer, Mary. *Signs of Cleopatra*. London: Routledge, 1993.

Hughes-Hallett, Lucy. *Cleopatra: Histories, Dreams and Distortions*. New York: Harper Collins, 1990.

Jones, Prudence J. *Cleopatra: A Sourcebook*. Norman: University of Oklahoma Press, 2006.

Kleiner, Diana E. E. *Cleopatra and Rome*. Cambridge: Harvard University Press, 2005.

Lichtheim, Miriam. *Ancient Egyptian Literature*. Los Angeles: University of California Press, 1980.

Miles, Margaret M., ed. *Cleopatra: A Sphinx Revisited*. Los Angeles: University of California Press, 2011.

Pomeroy, Sarah B. *Goddesses, Whores, Wives, and Slaves: Women in Classical Antiquity*. New York: Schocken, 1975.

Pushkin, Alexander. "Egyptian Nights." In *Novels, Tales, Journals: The Complete Prose of Alexander Pushkin*. Trans. Richard Pevear and Larissa Volokhonsky. New York: Knopf, 2016.

Rackin, Phyllis. "Shakespeare's Boy Cleopatra, the Decorum of Nature, and the Golden World of Poetry." *PMLA* 87, no. 2 (March 1972): 201–212.

Roller, Duane W. *Cleopatra: A Biography*. New York: Oxford University Press, 2010.

Rowlandson, Jane. *Women and Society in Greek and Roman Egypt: A Sourcebook*. Cambridge: Cambridge University Press, 1998.

Schiff, Stacy. *Cleopatra: A Life*. New York: Little, Brown, 2010.

Shakespeare, William. *Antony and Cleopatra*. Ed. Maynard Mack. Baltimore: Penguin, 1960.

Steppat, Michael. *The Critical Reception of Shakespeare's "Antony and Cleopatra" from 1607 to 1905*. Amsterdam: Verlag B. R. Grüner, 1980.

Tarn, W. W., and M. P. Charlesworth. *Octavian, Antony and Cleopatra*. Cambridge: Cambridge University Press, 1965.

Walker, Susan, and Peter Higgs. *Cleopatra of Egypt: From History to Myth*. Princeton: Princeton University Press, 2001.

Bibliography

Wanger, Walter. *My Life with Cleopatra: The Making of a Hollywood Classic.* New York: Vintage, 2013.

Wellendorf, Heather. "Ptolemy's Political Tool: Religion." *Studia Antiqua* 6, no. 1 (2008): 33–38.

Acknowledgments

I consulted several translations of Plutarch. The most recent and (for me) useful translation, and the one I quote from, is *The Age of Caesar: Five Roman Lives,* translated by Pamela Mensch and edited by James Romm, my friend and colleague at Bard College. I am grateful to him for inviting me to contribute to this series, and for giving me a reason to read not only Plutarch but Suetonius, Cassius Dio, Julius Caesar, Diodorus Siculus, and a few surviving Ptolemaic texts. With their quirks and prejudices, their gifts for storytelling and observation, these writers became my companions during the isolation imposed by Covid-19 and its long, snowy winter.

Index

Index

Index

on Cleopatra's first meeting with Caesar, 51–52; on Cleopatra's relationship with Caesar, 64–65; on the murder of Pompey, 45–47; on Romans' disapproval of Cleopatra, 68–69

Cassius Longinus, Gaius, 75, 78, 83

Charlesworth, M. P., 14; *Octavian, Antony and Cleopatra*, 99

Chauveau, Michel, 22–23

Chigi, Agostino, 68

Cicero, and Mark Antony, 69, 79, 81, 83, 84

Cleopatra (1917 film), 161–164; costumes in, 162

Cleopatra (1934 film), 164–168

Cleopatra (1963 film), 100, 157, 164, 165, 167, 168–176; budget for, 170

Cleopatra I, 30

Cleopatra III, 28

Cleopatra V Tryphaena, 38

Cleopatra VII, 34; accomplishments of, 5–6, 9, 13–15, 43–44, 77–78, 99–100; as adviser to Antony, 108, 111–112; and Antony, 1–2, 4, 6–7, 9–10, 11, 12, 13, 65, 66, 76, 78, 80, 83, 86–89; and Antony's conflict with Octavian, 107–109, 112–113; and Antony's death, 127–128; after Antony's defeat at Actium, 111–112, 116–118; Antony's fixation on, 95–96, 97–98, 103, 109, 110; as Antony's lover, 90–92, 102–103, 105–106; appearance of, 12–13, 130–131; after the Battle of Actium, 115–116; burial of, 137; and Caesar's assassination, 71, 74, 76, 77–78; Caesar's attraction to, 4, 11, 13; children of, 4, 65, 66–67, 91, 97, 105–106, 137–140; and concerns for her children following Antony's death, 130; death of, 4–5, 132–134; as depicted by classical authors, 9–12; as depicted in art, 9, 50, 87, 118–119, 134–136, 144–145; difficult choices faced by, 117–118; diverse accounts of her relationship with Caesar, 63–66; and the Donations of Alexandria, 105–107; and experimentation with poisons, 118–120; family background of, 4, 38–39; famine during reign of, 41–42, 77; as a feminist story, 5–7; film depictions of, 52–56, 161–177; and first meeting with Caesar, 49–52, 54–55; and the Gabiniani, 43–44; gods and goddesses worshipped by, 42; as Isis, 23–24, 42, 105, 131; legend of, after her death, 140, 176–177; and love triangle with Antony and Octavia, 1–2, 90–92, 102–103; Lucan's portrayal of, 52; as a Macedonian Greek, 8; motivations of, quesioned by historians, 3; Octavian's negotiations with, following Antony's death, 130–132; Octavian's overtures to, following Antony's defeat, 123–124; pearl earring as focus of stories about, 143–145; Plutarch's depiction of, 1–3, 6–7, 9–10, 12, 49, 50, 64–65, 79, 88; and Pompey, 44–45; as queen, 14–15, 38, 39, 42–44, 63, 96; and rift with Antony, 126; Romans' antipathy toward, 105–107, 109; as seductress, 8–9, 11–13, 87, 91, 100, 102, 103; siblings of, 38–39; stories inspired by, 14, 143–147; suicide of, 120, 131–134; territory ceded to her by Antony, 96; as threat to the Roman Empire, 69; tombs and mausoleums built by, 66, 124; visit to Rome by, 67–70; at war with Ptolemy XIII, 47, 56–59

Index

Index

Index

Index